P9-CQA-529

A Gift for

Withdrawn

_____

Presented by

_____

The
Queen's
English

The Queen's English

An A to Zed Guide to Distinctively British Words

C. J. MOORE

Reader's
Digest

The Reader's Digest Association, Inc.
New York, NY / Montreal

A READER'S DIGEST BOOK

Copyright © 2011 Elwin Street Limited

Conceived and produced by Elwin Street Limited, 144 Liverpool Road, London
N1 1LA, UK www.elwinstreet.com

Illustrator: Emma Farrarons

FOR READER'S DIGEST

U.S. Project Editor: Barbara Booth
Cover Designer: Jennifer Tokarski
Project Production Coordinator: Rich Kershner
Senior Art Director: George McKeon
Executive Editor, Trade Publishing: Dolores York
Manufacturing Manager: Elizabeth Dinda
Associate Publisher, Trade Publishing: Rosanne McManus
President and Publisher, Trade Publishing: Harold Clarke

Library of Congress Cataloging in Publication Data
Moore, C. J. (Christopher J.)
 The Queen's English : an A to Zed guide to distinctively British words / Christopher J. Moore.
    p. cm. -- (A Reader's Digest book)
 ISBN 978-1-60652-325-4
1. English language--Great Britain--Dictionaries. 2. English language--Great
Britain--Terms and phrases--Dictionaries. 3. English language--Great Britain--
Usage. 4. Great Britain--Civilization--Dictionaries. I. Title.
 PE1704.M58 2011
 427--dc22

                              2011009981

Reader's Digest is committed to both the quality of our products and the
service we provide to our customers. We value your comments, so please feel free to
contact us: The Reader's Digest Association, Inc., Adult Trade Publishing,
44 S. Broadway, White Plains, NY 10601

For more Reader's Digest products and information, visit our website:

www.rd.com (in the United States)

www.readersdigest.ca (in Canada)

Printed in the United States of America

1 3 5 7 9 10 8 6 4 2

"We have really everything in common with America nowadays except, of course, language."
—*Oscar Wilde*

Contents

Introduction

The Queen's English. What a noble phrase! The expression speaks of centuries of history and worldwide political and social influence, not to mention a long and deeply felt aspect of the English character. For the Queen's English is not just a language like any other. Over the years, it has represented a virtual institution, a Royal Academy without the actual academy. It stands proudly but invisibly at the center of a global culture, yet with doors as solid as the Bank of England's, offering entry to some, refusing it to others. Many a poor soul has been shown the way out for little more than twanging a vowel or splitting an infinitive.

What is the Queen's English?

Although the Queen rules over the United Kingdom of Great Britain and Northern Ireland, as well as being constitutional monarch of various Commonwealth countries, the Queen's English refers only to a language derived from, or aspiring to be like, what is spoken in England. So for the purposes of this book, we lay aside the rich linguistic peculiarities of Scotland, Wales, and Ireland to delve into the characters of the English themselves.

The Queen's English is the standard form of English spoken in the south of England. It is the Golden Rule above all other dialects and deviations. Yet part of the fascination is exploring the assaults upon it. Nowadays people are proud of their regional dialects and local accents. This A to Zed guide will dig out the lynchpins of the system and reveal why this language seems to be a sacred temple preserving a culture only for those with the birth and education to qualify. Or, as some might say, the pompous domain of a self-appointed upper- and middle-class club of snobs and busybodies, anxious to keep out the hoi polloi, commoners, upstarts, the incoherent, ignorant, misguided, and ungrammatical masses.

One thing is for sure: As soon as you open your mouth, your listener puts you into a social category. "Language most shewes a man: speake that I may see thee," wrote the playwright Ben Jonson as early as 1641.

How it all came about

Respecting what once began as the King's English was already established by the mid-seventeenth century, and we have to go back some 200 years to find where it all started. In the Middle Ages, Latin and French had been the languages of government and diplomacy, but in the Renaissance period the change to vernacular languages was happening all over Europe, and England was no exception. As yet, English had little or no standard spelling and existed in a thousand different varieties and dialects.

Only around the start of the fifteenth century did a standard form of English become adopted for government business in London, thus establishing a "court" English as opposed to a "country" English. When William Caxton set up his printing press later in that century, this was the standard he adopted, initiating an industry so successful that here we are, still at it, making books.

As for the expression "King's English," Thomas Wilson appears to have been the first one to use it, in his *Art of Rhetorique of 1553,* where he takes to task the pretensions of those who infect the English language with fancy foreign borrowings, or what he calls "strange inkhorn terms."

Over the next three centuries, driven by their annoyance with lax standards, many other writers published guides and norms for good writing and speaking, and educationalists soon followed suit.

The struggle for a unified, elegant tongue

The idea of the King's English took a real blow with the accession to the throne in 1714 of George I, a 54-year-old Hanoverian prince who ruled for 13 years without ever learning to speak English. Perhaps dismayed by this unfortunate need to borrow foreign kings and queens, the English middle and upper classes showed more and more fervor for a national identity and culture. Language was increasingly the key that opened the door to elegant society, employment, and advancement. Lessons in elocution—the art of speaking properly—became a necessary part of a young lady's education, especially those in search of a husband with grand estates and incomes.

Perhaps the most famous example of the social power of "received" English is found in the 1960s stage musical and film *My Fair Lady.* In the opening scene, Eliza Doolittle, a Cockney flower girl, encounters the mother of a young man, who asks her how the girl knows her son:

Eliza: Ow, eez ye-ooa san, is e? Wal, fewd dan y' deooty bawmz a mather should, eed now bettern to spawl a pore gel's flahrzn than ran awy athaht pyin. Will ye-oo py me f'them?

Eliza, painfully aware of her dreadful Cockney accent, goes to see Henry Higgins, a professor of phonetics, to ask him for elocution lessons. The professor, stirred on by a bet with a friend, takes on the challenge of changing the flower girl's speech and manners to make her acceptable to upper-class London society.

Embracing a new linguistic freedom

Postwar English society brought on new linguistic theories, banishing the insistence on "correctness." From then on, all varieties of language became new hunting grounds, and linguists raced about cataloging dialects and tongues, the rarer and more threatened the better. Society and education moved rapidly with this change in attitude. Added to the new linguistic freedoms was that of ignorance, since grammar was no longer taught in schools.

The BBC, slow to change but wanting to keep its listeners happy, started recruiting local radio DJs off the street to showcase their local accents, jokes, and rapid-fire wit. Accents became the new cachet, attractively packaged to represent real-live people rather than social constructs. Among the shifts in perception, a national bank discovered that its telephone clients seemed to trust a Scottish accent more than any other, and so it was to be.

Linguists gave the English the freedom to speak as they like, and by golly, they took the opportunity! As a result, perhaps at no time since the first Elizabethan period, when Shakespeare took full advantage of it, has the language been in such a state of rapid and creative change. The sheer inventiveness of English is what captures the imagination, and in the following pages, we shall see just how far they have tested the limits.

Aga

An aga—an unusual and extremely expensive type of domestic oven—represents the ideal of home comfort and convenience for the English and has become an iconic piece of equipment for a certain type of English household.

There is something of a mystery here as to why the aga's inventor, the Swede Gustaf Dalén (1869–1937), already rich and famous as a 1912 Nobel Laureate for Physics, went to the trouble of designing it for his own kitchen. It seems that Dalén was fascinated with devising ways of making equipment more energy efficient. So perhaps it was the same obsession that induced him to develop a heavy-duty cast-iron cooking range that could run for 24 hours off 8 pounds (3.5 kg) of solid fuel, producing an intense and permanent radiant heat. According to some, he had been blinded from an accident and wanted an oven that had no buttons or controls.

Now more than 80 years old, the aga is under British ownership and, with its enthusiastic adoption by middle-class households, has acquired an essentially English character. Famous chefs have pinned their recommendations to it. It has even inspired a modern genre of novel known as the Aga-Saga (typified by the work

of the writer Joanna Trollope), which explores the existence of middle-class suburban families (similar to WASPs), their domestic life, passions, and temptations.

None of this tells you what the actual appeal of an aga is and why owners fall hopelessly in love with it. You will just have to find someone who owns one and ask. Just make sure you allow plenty of time for the long, detailed, and enthusiastic reply.

All mouth and trousers

This expression is well known in the north of England as a woman's crushing remark about any man with over-sized ideas about himself. "Mouth" refers to brash talk, and "trousers" is the English name for pants. The grammarian's term for this kind of phrase, where the container stands for the thing contained, is metonymy. What is interesting in this case is the implication that pants in themselves—or actually, the men inside them—have a negative quality. One might have thought that such a feminist attitude is a modern invention, but far from it. The robust women of the north of England have long been conducting their own battle with male chauvinism.

However, the phrase has spread throughout all of England and has gone through a curious transformation, a process known to linguists as spontaneous change. The obvious negative of "trousers" has corrupted the expression into "All mouth and no trousers," a form in which it now frequently appears. This seems to have come about by false analogy with a whole lot of phrases using the form "All this and no that..."—such as "All talk and no action," "All bread and no cheese," "All bark and no bite." What is amusing here is that the corrupted version of the saying has unwittingly restored a positive value to pants.

All right

If there is one thing the English are famous for, it's understatement. This particular quirk is an endless source of confusion for Americans, who prefer plain speaking or, as in the case of the monosyllabic cowboy, very little speech at all. The habit of understatement is clearly inherited, for if you ask a very small English child what their school is like, you will almost certainly get the answer, "All right." This answer cannot possibly have been learned at anyone's knee and must be an acquired

English characteristic passed on genetically, thus disproving Darwinian theory at a stroke.

That same child will go through life answering "All right" to all sorts of questions, ranging from "What was the weather like?" to, we must suppose, "What did you think of your funeral service?"

Anorak

In its original sense, an anorak is a piece of weatherproof clothing, usually with a hood and drawstrings, apparently copied from a type of Inuit clothing in the arctic region. But in its widely used slang meaning, an anorak is a person obsessively engaged in a detailed activity of absolutely no interest to "normal" people. The association probably came from the fact that trainspotters—people who stand for hours at railroad stations collecting the engine numbers of locomotives as they pass—usually wore warm outdoor clothing of an anorak type.

The slack, sloppy appearance of the anorak garment, as far removed from elegance and sophistication as can be imagined, came to represent the supposedly rather dull and unimaginative personality of the wearer. No doubt this is an extremely unfair generalization, but anyone who has found himself trapped in a railway car with an anorak, as I was on the occasion of the final journey of an old steam locomotive, might well reach such a conclusion.

Anoraks appear in public life, too. The British prime minister John Major (1990–97) was considered by the media to be a gray and colorless individual, and one famous cartoon shows him as a trainspotter's anorak—far

from the illustrations that
depict Catherine Middleton,
Duchess of Cambridge, who
is well on her way to being the
next global style icon. She has
already been listed on Britain's
Best Dressed List and on the
International Best Dressed
List. You won't catch her in
an anorak, unless it's by Issa
London, one of her favorite designers (*see also* "Naff").

Anticlockwise

No, the English have nothing against
clocks. It's simply their way of saying
counterclockwise.

Argy-bargy

This funny little term, both noun and verb, refers to a
minor quarrel or spat. It's not as common as it once was,
and it has a more innocent ring to it than what nowadays might be called "aggro," a popular English term
meaning aggravation. It is probably a corruption of the
Scottish phrase "argle-bargle," which we find in Robert
Louis Stevenson's *Kidnapped* (1886).

Many popular words have a similar dual structure, a
feature of languages all over the world, possibly related to a
baby's first attempts at talking. A word double can be cre-

ated either by simply repeating the term (bye–bye, no–no) or by rhyming with or echoing it (honey-bunny, dingle-dangle). The result is fun, expressive, and very creative.

As pleased as Punch

English people of a certain age will remember the childish pleasures of summertime at fairs and at the beach, which always included the Punch and Judy puppet show. The appallingly wicked behavior of Mr. Punch, beating all around with his stick, would raise shrieks of laughter, matched only by the squeals when the crocodile popped up with its terrible jaws. The association "as pleased as" arises from the fact that the grotesque figure of Punch wears a permanent grin and is delighted with his own wickedness.

The tradition goes way back, at least to the seventeenth century, originating in the Italian puppet shows of Punchinello, or Polichinello, which spread all over Europe. The entertainment came to England around 1662, when London diarist Samuel Pepys noted a repeated visit to a show that "pleased me mightily."

Modern political correctness has dealt a severe blow to this kind of diversion, for after all, we cannot have children thinking that violence is the solution to everything (*see also* "Oh, yes, he did!").

At sixes and sevens

Personally, I am all at sixes and sevens about this saying, which means being in a state of complete disorder or disagreement. Nobody seems to have a clear idea of where it comes from, but the favorite explanation is that it comes from Chaucer's *Troilus and Criseyde,* around 1375, where he writes "to set the world on six and seven." Two centuries later, in *Richard II,* Shakespeare has the Duke of York saying, "All is uneven, and everything is left at six and seven." By the eighteenth century, dictionaries had arrived at the present form of "at sixes and sevens."

Theorists have leaped at any combination of six and seven in literature, from the Bible onward, to find some consistent root for the saying. After long research, I can only conclude that the real basis of the saying comes from the modern English author Douglas Adams's revelation that the answer to the mystery of life, the universe, and everything is 42—namely, seven sixes, or six sevens, however you want to see it.

Scientists, including the great Richard Feynman, have gone on to demonstrate the extraordinary presence of the number 42 in cosmic mathematics. This is so utterly puzzling that it must leave all of us at sixes and sevens.

Baker's dozen

Whereas a normal dozen is 12, a baker's dozen is 13, and for the following reason. Selling under the proper weight must have been an age-old practice, and we find that most ancient civilizations imposed standard weights and measures in order to make regular and reliable trade possible. The Romans, in particular, established their own standards in Britain, which lasted for centuries after they had gone. The English measurements of pounds, ounces, pence, and miles all originated in Roman measures, though many Saxon standards were kept in use as well, especially for land ownership.

For day-to-day trading purposes, medieval guilds maintained their own standards and ensured that their traders honored them. One basic product that lent itself to cheating was bread, as it is hard to make loaves of a consistent size and weight. So at least as early as the thirteenth century, the bakers' guild—the Worshipful Company of Bakers—introduced the practice of adding a little extra "in-bread" to the loaf sold in order to ensure they were not selling underweight, for which the punishment was severe. For the same reason, when selling bread in bulk to

other traders, they added a thirteenth loaf to every 12 sold.
Thus, 13 loaves became known as a baker's dozen.

Balderdash

An exclamation of mysterious origin but traceable as far
back as 1596, this spluttering word originally referred to a
jumbled mix of liquors. By 1674 it meant a senseless col-
lection of words and general nonsense or noise, and in the
eighteenth century it entered Samuel Johnson's dictionary
as "a rude mixture." One may safely draw the conclusion
that the educated English mind, with its respect for common sense, order, and logic, has little patience with
arguments that are patently nonsense.

Bangers 'n' mash

Fortunate children all over the world grow
up remembering the good,
comforting food served at
the family table, symbolic
of nourishment and secu-
rity. For English children
bangers 'n' mash is one of
those memorable meals, like
fish 'n' chips, but much more associated
with home cooking than with **takeaway**★ food.

Bangers is a slang word for sausages, going back at
least a hundred years, and of uncertain origin but proba-

★*Words in boldface indicate entries within this book.*

bly a reference to their shape. Mash in this case is mashed potatoes, though more widely this word can be used to mean any vegetable or cereal mashed up with hot water, originally as feed for animals.

Every family used to have its favorite recipe for this simple dish, either in the ingredients for the rich onion gravy usually poured over it, or in the preparation of the mash.

If bangers 'n' mash isn't your cup of tea, perhaps you'd prefer bubble and squeak, an old English breakfast dish made from frying up leftover greens and potato, or toad-in-a-hole, which is basically Yorkshire pudding with sausages cooked in it. Lunch might be a sarnies (sandwiches) on white or brown (never whole wheat) bread, or cheese and bread (see "Ploughman's Lunch"). What's afterward? That would be dessert, likely to be called a pudding. A pudding can be any type of dessert, including a jelly (Jell-O to Americans), biscuits, or spotted dick, a suet pudding with dried fruit served with a custard sauce.

Barmy

Another way of saying crazy, insane, foolish, or mad. For instance, "You would have to be barmy to go out in the pouring rain without your **wellies**!" This term first came up in the sixteenth century in a literal sense meaning "foaming," leading to why the English refer to the head on their beer as barm. By 1602 "barmy" was being used to describe someone acting in an agitated or irrational way, as if their head were filled with froth.

Biscuit

This is a cracker or a thin cookie in England, much different from the biscuits in America, which refer to a small roll. The confusion today actually goes back to the origin of the word. In Middle French the word *bescuit* means "twice cooked." Biscuits were originally cooked in a twofold process, whereby they were baked and then dried out in an oven, forming a hard cookie or cracker. In England, stores carry all sorts of assorted biscuits for cheese.

Blackball

This phrase, meaning to exclude or shun, comes from a background that is quintessentially English and is intimately linked to its long-established systems of privilege.

Traditionally, a certain proof of a gentleman's social standing was the London clubs to which he belonged. In the past these were all-male preserves, and to join, a candidate had to be sponsored by an existing member. The practice was to vote in secret, using a bag into which the members one by one put a colored ball (yes) or a black ball (no.) Then the balls were counted. In some institutions one black ball was sufficient to exclude the candidate; in others it had to be a majority. Either way, membership was denied, and the candidate was "blackballed."

English society being what it is, the fact of being blackballed by a club was enough to cast a severe shadow over someone's character. Few would think it likely that the black ball was merely the fruit of another gentleman's envy or vindictiveness. Gentlemen don't behave like that, do they?

Black dog

This vivid term for dark depression has a special English connection; Britain's Second World War leader Sir Winston Churchill used it to refer to his own black moods. To realize that he suffered extreme moods of this kind sheds an ironic light on his personality, when we consider that as prime minister in such difficult times, his fame rested on his constant ability to inspire and raise the spirits of the whole nation.

The association of a black dog with bad luck and misfortune goes back to classical times and recurs often in folklore as a symbol of a threatening presence.

Blinkered

When someone has a limited viewpoint or is very narrow-minded, they are described as blinkered or having a blinkered position. "She loves classical music and is blinkered when it comes to any other genre." This originated in 1867 and came from the blinkers that carriage-pulling horses wore to limit their vision so they wouldn't be distracted or startled if they saw something in their side view. As a result, they could only see in one direction—straight ahead.

Bloomsbury

Bloomsbury is an upscale part of central London around the British Museum, once characterized by Georgian-period squares and known for its bookshops, publishing houses, and social elegance. But the devastation dealt—

first by Second World War bombings and then in the 1970s by London University in its quest for charmless concrete utility buildings—has left the area a pale shadow of what it once was.

Yet echoes of a more elegant, if risqué, past are still heard. The so-called Bloomsbury Set in London has something of the same notoriety as the literary and artistic Americans who congregated in Paris around the 1920s and proceeded to scandalize everyone with their unconventional lifestyle. Publisher Leonard Woolf, as an undergraduate at Cambridge, had already established relations with an elite group of young intellectuals known as the Apostles, and later with his wife, novelist Virginia Woolf. He went on to maintain a close-knit circle of like-minded thinkers and artists centered on Gordon Square, where Virginia lived.

The inner circle included Duncan Grant, Vanessa Bell, Lytton Strachey, Roger Fry, Clive Bell, and the economist John Maynard Keynes, though many others stopped by to share in the avant-garde buzz surrounding the group, given added attraction by their effortlessly superior social standing. But the elitist ambience of the group, their progressive politics, and their disregard for convention—especially in personal and sexual relationships—gave grounds for much criticism, leading to the dismissive comment that the group did little more than "live in squares and love in triangles."

Bluestocking

Since the eighteenth century, both English society and literature have been strongly influenced by women's struggle to be recognized for their intelligence as well as their beauty and needlework skills. So it must be all the more discouraging for women that the label "bluestocking," referring mostly nowadays to female academics or intellectuals, should still have a negative ring to it rather than approval and affirmation.

But perhaps it was always so. The term came into use in London in the 1750s with the creation of a literary discussion group by high-society ladies wanting to follow the example of French *salons,* often hosted by influential aristocratic women, as well as the French women's group known as *Bas bleu.* The English group may well have referred to themselves informally as the Blue Stocking Society, but an early use of the name seems to have come dismissively from one of the ladies' husbands who was not at all impressed with his wife's friends and their literary pretensions.

Why the French should have been able to establish such a strong *salon* tradition led by women, while English female society was left struggling for intellectual equality with men, reflects a certain difference between the two cultures of the time. English women went on to plead their case mainly through the medium of the novel, in which the inequality and injustice experienced by women at all levels of society were described in vivid terms. As the famous and pithy quote from Jane Austen's *Northanger Abbey* goes, "A woman especially, if she have the misfortune of knowing anything, should conceal it as well as she can" (*see also* "Sentiments").

Bob

There are many expressions for British money. Before decimalization in 1971, which introduced the simple, lackluster "p" for new pence, it was the age of pounds, shilling, pence, and many other colorful words for British coins, such as florins, half-crowns, pennies, bobs, tanners, and thrupenny bits.

A pound comprised 20 shillings, commonly called a bob. Two bobs would be 10 pence. The origin of bob isn't known for sure, but it dates back to the late 1700s. According to the Brewer's 1870 Dictionary of Phrase and Fable, "bob" could be derived from "bawbee," which was sixteenth-century slang for a half-penny.

Bobby

Any visitor to Britain should know the best way to address a police officer. After all, you never know when you might need help. But there are so many slang words for them, ranging from the rather outdated bobby or copper to more recent terms, like the fuzz and the bill, that it starts to get a bit confusing. So let's start from the beginning.

"Bobby" is a very old-fashioned and endearing term for the English police, dating from the early nineteenth century when Sir Robert "Bob" Peel introduced the first police force to London. In the capital they were also once known as peelers. Traditionally, the bobby was a figure of local support and help, belonging to a time when parents always said to children: "If you're ever in trouble, ask a policeman." In more modern times "the fuzz," "the bill," or "the old bill," in general use, also seem to be acceptable.

Sadly, the bobby image of the police has suffered since the 1960s when, instead of setting up a separate semi-military force for crowd control, as in many other European countries, the government hired ordinary policemen to don armor and weapons and bash the rioting English into submission. Since then, more unpleasant terms for the police, especially among the young, have included "pigs" or "the filth."

The police have struggled hard to regain their community image, but even now they give mixed messages. It is not unusual to see a heavily armed policeman wearing a bullet-proof jacket, with aggressive equipment of every type strapped to his chest and belt, and a large label on his back reading COMMUNITY POLICE.

So how would I address a police officer in the street? I think in practice I would just be polite and avoid any form of address.

Bob's your uncle

This phrase refers to any task that can be accomplished neatly and simply with a kind of one-two-three precision, the final result always being "And Bob's your uncle." The expression naturally lends itself to all sorts of silly and disbelieving replies, such as "And Fanny's my aunt."

Its supposed origin was the appointment of Arthur Balfour, nephew of the Victorian prime minister Robert

Cecil, Lord Salisbury, to be chief secretary for Ireland in 1887, an office for which no one, other than Uncle Robert, thought he had any useful qualifications at all. So he got the job purely because Bob was his uncle. A nice theory, and no one has come up with anything convincingly better.

Boot

Much the way American boots protect wearers from the elements, a boot of an automobile protects its contents from weather damage. A boot in British terminology is the luggage compartment of a car, which in the old days had an apron or cover (of leather or rubber) to protect its contents from rain or mud. The term originated in the days of stagecoaches, when the area for baggage at each side of the coach was called a boot.

Sounds funny, but what do elephants have to do with automobiles in America?

Bottoms up

When it was England's turn to rule the world and she needed a lot of ships and men to run around policing it, there was a constant call for recruitment to the navy. But persuading healthy young men to join up was not an easy task, so trickery was relied upon. So-called "press gangs" went around dockside pubs and bought drinks for the unwary. The trick was that at the bottom of the pewter pot was a coin, and on finishing the drink, you automatically "took the King's shilling," thus agreeing to join up (though somewhat by force as they dragged you away).

As people became aware of this trap, pubs began to sell drink in glass-bottomed pewter pots to make the coin visible. So as you lifted the tankard, you could then see the coin against the glass bottom. Hence, the expression "Bottoms up," which continues to be used as a happy exhortation to drink up.

Bowdlerize

A certain Thomas Bowdler (1754–1825), who had retired from being a doctor and clearly had nothing better to do, decided to edit the works of Shakespeare in order to make them suitable for family reading. His *Family Shakespeare* appeared in 1818, with the necessary cuts, including the entire deletion of characters that he thought too bawdy altogether. This prudish kind of editing has since been known as "bowdlerizing," arising out of the strict morality that is generally referred to as "Victorian values."

British bulldog

The British bulldog motif is familiar to every tourist visiting London, and it evokes, yet again, the image the English have of themselves as resilient, strong, and, when provoked, having a nasty bite. The national self-image is all the more confirmed when we consider that Sir Winston Churchill, that famous wartime leader, was as close in looks to a human bulldog as one can possibly imagine.

The same cannot be said of Margaret Thatcher, with whom Churchill comparisons are often made. But then, after being ruthlessly stabbed in the back by her

Cabinet colleagues in November 1990 and thrown ignominiously out of Number 10 Downing Street, she did allow herself a tear, which was caught on camera. Perhaps she simply wasn't of the bulldog breed, after all.

By hook or by crook

It is nice to find a common phrase that goes back as far as this one and which seems to link back to England's feudal past.

In medieval times, when the peasantry were not allowed to cut down trees, they were still permitted to gather firewood from loose or dead branches that could be obtained using a "hook" (bill hook, a traditional cutting tool) or "crook," a staff with a curved end. No doubt the desperate peasant often exceeded the strict use of these tools, and so the sense is to achieve something by whatever means possible. The first recorded use of the phrase is from the fourteenth century. Some aspects of human nature certainly remain unchanged.

Car park

An area where people park their cars, of course. Isn't that obvious? This certainly is not one of the more clever English terms, but there is a legendary story in England centered around a car park in Bristol. Apparently, two years ago a Bristol Zoo car park attendant gained worldwide attention after the Bristol *Times* reported that for 23 years he had been imposing as an employee for the car park. Every day he collected, on average, 400 pounds ($560), lining his own pockets with the cash, and then one day simply vanished. It was estimated that when he finally "retired," he had collected nearly 3.6 million pounds ($7 million).

The news report circulated the globe via the Internet, and calls flooded the Bristol Zoo from people wanting to know more. After investigation, it was found that this tale was no more than an urban legend, created by the Bristol *Times* themselves.

Chalk and cheese

Philosophers, and not only English ones, spend their time telling us what we can and cannot do logically. You can't compare things as different as chalk and cheese. Or can you? What at first sight could be simpler than the idea behind this common expression, meaning that two people or objects are as far apart in kind as is possible? In philosopher language they belong to different categories. Similar expressions of one kind or another are widely found around the world. If it isn't chalk and cheese, it is apples and oranges, apples and pears, carrots and potatoes, or more colorfully, in the case of Serbians, grandmothers and toads.

In the fourteenth-century *Confessio Amantis* of John Gower, we find the suggestion that some shopkeeper was adulterating his wares, such that "ful ofte chalk for cheese he changeth with ful littel cost." Now if the two things really were "as different as chalk and cheese," surely someone would have noticed. It seems more probable that the phrase connecting chalk and cheese originally implied a certain obtuseness on the part of the observer, as in "He can't tell chalk from cheese." Indeed, Michael Quinion reports: "By the sixteenth century the phrase had become a fixed expression. Hugh Latimer wrote rather sarcastically around 1555: 'As though I could not discern cheese from chalk.'"

Later, in the seventeenth century, it may well have been that the English Civil War produced the clear distinction between the valley "cheese people" (Parliamentarians) and Dorset downs "chalk people" (Royalists). The phrase "chalk and cheese" is still widely used to refer to rural Dorset.

More recently, academic thinkers have cast doubt in our minds on the whole question of sameness and difference. Take apples and oranges. What, the linguists say, is a "golden apple," that magical and mythical fruit of antiquity and legend, if it isn't an orange? Well, another plausible theory would say it was a tomato, but that doesn't have exactly the same ring to it. I can't see the classical hero, Paris, offering a goddess a tomato.

Adding the weight of medical authority to this debate, the *British Medical Journal* published an important study by Stamford surgeon James Barone in December 2000, entitled "Comparing apples and oranges: a randomised prospective study," where the author concludes that:

> ... apples and oranges are not only comparable; indeed they are quite similar. The admonition 'Let's not compare apples with oranges' should be replaced immediately with a more appropriate expression such as 'Let's not compare walnuts with elephants' or 'Let's not compare tumour necrosis factor with linguini.'

Cheeky

Cheeky means you are glib, disrespectful, or rude, but crafty at the same time. For instance, you would be considered a bit cheeky if you have an answer for everything or you give someone a backhanded compliment. Someone who is cheeky would say something like, "I love your dress. It reminds me of the wallpaper I had in my kitchen once."

Cheers

One of the most common words in England. It's not only used in pubs just before downing a drink with friends but also when being handed your drink and when leaving the pub, for it also means thank you and good-bye! With all this "cheering," it's nice to know the British government just unveiled a shatterproof pint glass.

Chelsea

No, not the English soccer team. We're talking about the annual Chelsea Flower Show, reputed to be the greatest flower show on Earth. It is a major event for all those Englishmen and women who have spent the entire year **pottering** (and probably potting, too) and who gather by the thousands to see the professional landscape designers compete against one another. Why the general public subjects itself to this experience of acute envy is not exactly clear.

Most amateur gardeners spend a great deal of time battling against the unexpected and the unwilling— weather, plants, neighbors, spouses. But there is one consolation found in coming to Chelsea. For it seems the professionals have precisely the same problems. Plants fail to thrive, water features dry up or overflow, neighbors complain, workmen don't turn up on time, trellises collapse in the wind...And still, in the end, the results turn out marvelous.

Yet a word of cautionary wisdom. The writer Rudyard

Kipling produced what may be the best practical comment on gardening in literature in a brief verse that goes:

Our England is a garden,
and such gardens are not made
by sighing, "Oh, how beautiful!"
and sitting in the shade.

Chips

The English love affair with fish and chips is deeply and permanently established, at least as long as there are fish in the sea. Long before McDonald's appeared on the English scene, they had **takeaway** fish-and-chip shops in almost every town and village in the country.

American travelers may find themselves mystified by their first encounter with a British fish-and-chip shop, because the chips in question are actually what

Americans know as French fries, a potato preparation that originated in Belgium. What Americans know as chips are what the British call "crisps."

Some social researchers have discovered the English can be "surprisingly patriotic and enthusiastic about the humble chip," in the words of anthropologist Kate Fox, who has dedicated her life to studying the strange ways of the English. Ironically, others report that the national dish is no longer fish and chips, but the Great British Curry—specifically, a variation on chicken tikka masala, which originated in the Indian subcontinent.

The humble chip has even entered literature, in Arnold Wesker's 1962 *Chips with Everything.* This is Wesker's semi-autobiographical story of a national service conscript, the son of a general, trying to fit in with his fellow conscripts of working-class background. He finds himself at odds both with them and with the officers with whom his own background should make him a natural ally. The dumbing-down formula of "chips with everything" reflects the tortured class relations so typical of English institutions and the impossible struggle of the young man to redefine his identity in his own right.

It is purely coincidental that English people describe someone abrasively living out the discomfort of being a social misfit as having a "chip on their shoulder."

Chivvy

To persuade someone to do something, especially if they don't really want to: "He chivvied me into driving him to the airport." It's also used frequently with "along,"

as in trying to hurry someone up. "Try to chivvy along
the children before we are too late." It can also mean
to harass, nag, or torment. This term originated in the
early 1900s from the expression "chevy chase," which
means "a running pursuit," which in turn came from the
"Ballad of Chevy Chase," a popular song that described a
hunting party on the borderland that turned into a battle
between the English and the Scots.

Continent, the

The English are very conscious of being an island race.
"On the Continent" is where everyone else in Europe
lives, on the other side of the English Channel. There
was purportedly once a famous London newspaper head-
line that read, FOG IN CHANNEL. CONTINENT CUT OFF.

In earlier centuries it was considered an essential ele-
ment of a young person's education to do the Grand Tour
of European cities, learning something of their neighbors'
artistic and cultural achievements in the process. Many
English travelers fell in love with these places. Some never
came back. But for most the experience was fairly mixed
and dangerously unhealthy. The strange food, the doubt-
ful purity of the water, the casual approach to life's little
intimacies were far too unfamiliar and uncomfortable,
even life-threatening, for those of a delicate temperament.
For such unsteady souls the white cliffs of Dover were well
and truly a beloved sight on the return home.

For these reasons, it could be said that the moment an
Englishman first stepped off a plane or boat and onto the
Continent, it was literally a turning point in his life.

Coventry, send someone to

Coventry is a businesslike English Midlands town that appears to have never done anyone any harm, yet to be sent there (according to this saying) is to be ostracized, ignored, shunned, or treated as a pariah. Where can such an idea have evolved?

Like so many sayings that enter popular language, this one has an uncertain origin. But it may have developed during the seventeenth-century English civil war between Royalists and Parliamentarians, when king's soldiers who were captured in the battles around the Midlands were literally sent to Coventry, a town that was loyal to Parliament. The people of Coventry were not very welcoming and tended to ignore the disgraced soldiers, who were not even served in taverns or inns and were largely reduced to begging in the streets. To be sent to Coventry may have served then as a threat hanging over Royalist soldiers so that they would fight all the harder to avoid capture.

But somehow the threat didn't have the required effect, and the Parliamentarians subsequently defeated and deposed the forces of King Charles I and, in 1649, cut off his head, sending shock waves throughout the royal courts of Europe. Many thought that at that moment, England had reached, in today's phrase, the end of the monarchy, but it was not to be.

Crumbs!

In certain circles, and certainly in children's literature, using four-letter words and taking the Lord's name in vain is to be avoided with simple exclamations of "Crumbs!" or even "Crikey," both euphemisms for Christ. Other exclamations include "dagnamit," "for Pete's sake," "by gosh," "cor blimey" (God blind me), and "gee whizz" (Jesus).

You might well have uttered "Crumbs!" if you had been witness to a recent event on the Dorsetshire coast, which attracted a good deal more than local interest. Half a mile of coastline simply collapsed into the sea. It was the biggest landslide in the area for a hundred years. Alarm bells went off all around the southeast coast. For the fact is, little England is steadily crumbling away into the sea and getting smaller and smaller. Two reasons: First, Britain as a geological structure is tipping slowly into the North Sea; second, global warming is raising sea levels.

Human arrogance is personified in ancient English history by the figure of King Canute, who pretended to try and stop a rising tide in order to teach his nobles a lesson. The nobles misunderstood completely, and the English inherited a belief that they could hold back the ocean forever. But there is growing recognition of the futility of such actions. The latest studies on coastal defenses now promote a different strategy: Give a certain amount of land back to the sea and retreat gracefully to a safe distance. Whole villages, some whose history goes back more than a thousand years, would be lost. The alternative would mean major towns and cities facing disastrous floods over the coming decades. "Crumbs! Crikey," I can hear the environment minister saying. "What do we do now?"

Curate's egg

The British are known for their diplomacy, and a humorous cartoon of 1895 playfully exhibits this common behavior, giving rise to the phrase "a bit of a curate's egg." In it a curate—that is, an assistant clergyman—is having breakfast with his bishop and is clearly in trouble as he eats his egg. The bishop says, "I'm afraid you have a bad egg, Mr. Jones," to which the poor man, anxious not to offend his superior, replies, "Oh, no, my Lord. I assure you that parts of it are excellent!"

So a "curate's egg" is therefore used to refer to something that, out of politeness, one does not wish to condemn openly, such as in a book review. "Like the curate's egg, good in parts" is a common use of the phrase.

Cut a dash

Or "cut a fine dash." Sometimes "cut a fine figure." The sense is clear: to appear in public dressed up in a way that is striking or, one might say, dashing.

But English is a very strange language sometimes. Imagine trying to explain to a class of English students the meaning of either "cut" or "dash" here. The dozens of other meanings bear no relation to showy dress, and we can only find echoes of sayings such as "the cut of his cloth." Brewer, in his *Dictionary of Phrase and Fable,* connects the phrase to the French *coup* (stroke) via "to make a masterly stroke."

Daft

This word originally meant mild and gentle, but in late
Middle English it turned into "stupid." More than likely
this is based on "daff," which means a simpleton or fool.
You can be called daft by someone who thinks you're
not being sensible, or if you are really crazy about something, like football, you could be daft about it.

Dickensian

The Victorian novelist Charles Dickens (1837–96) wrote
graphically and emotionally about the social conditions in
the London of his day. The accounts in his novels of the
appalling fate of the poor, and the squalid conditions in pris-
ons and poorhouses, attracted much attention and increased
public awareness of the terrible suffering endured by the
lowest classes of society with no social welfare systems or
services. Nowadays the term Dickensian is still used to
describe acute conditions of poverty or deprivation wherever they may be found in Britain.

Disgusted (of Tunbridge Wells)

It is not unusual for retired military men and women, colonels and air vice marshals and the like, to find it hard to adapt to their new unemployed status. They have to fill their days with useful things to do, mindful of a disciplined childhood and the eternal words of Rudyard Kipling's poem "If":

If you can fill the unforgiving minute
With sixty seconds' worth of distance run,
Yours is the Earth and everything that's in it,
And—which is more—you'll be a Man, my son!

Regardless of this inspired advice, normal men and women may subside into creative inactivity after a lifetime of hard grind. But not our retired colonel. After an early breakfast—for he will continue to get up between 6:00 and 7:00 A.M. as he has done all his life—he picks up his pen and writes to his daily newspaper. This is likely to be *The Times* or *Daily Telegraph*—newspapers that he still believes, despite all of the evidence, hold the same values as himself.

Now the colonel's trained powers of observation have made him notice that the world is not as it was. All around are signs of social degeneration, depraved youth, litter, and the incompetence of local authorities, not to mention single mothers and feral infants. "The center will not hold; things fall apart," the colonel cries to himself, and dashes off yet another letter of protest, describing the objects of his contempt in clinical detail. Afraid of drawing unwelcome attention to himself, he signs the letter: "Disgusted (of Tunbridge Wells)."

No one is sure whether the colonel really existed. But a succession of complaints signed in this way appears to have been published by the *Tunbridge Wells Advertiser* in the 1950s, possibly in a desperate editorial attempt to fill the Letters column.

It is true that the colonel's reactionary attitude seems to fit this fairly quiet and elegant southern town, a spa once favored by royalty (hence, the Royal in its official name). The novelist E. M. Forster displayed the image of the town in his 1908 novel *A Room with a View,* when his character Miss Bartlett says: "I am used to Tunbridge Wells, where we are all hopelessly behind the times."

DIY

Elsewhere we examine the national English hobby of **pottering**, an activity that requires absolutely no skill at all and appeals to England's love of all that is amateur. To talk of being good at pottering, or bad at it, would be nonsense. However, bolder Englishmen who have retained memories of their jungle-hunting days and feel the need to flex their muscles are drawn toward DIY, or Do-It-Yourself. They are drawn for economic reasons, too, because a good plumber—who earns more annually than the prime minister—will charge a huge amount to come out and clear a sink, a job that will take him about two minutes.

So the argument for DIY is clear. But beware, because once an Englishman falls into the trap of thinking he can do anything with tools, he is lost. First, he will probably end up spending more on the tools and equipment than he ever did on the plumbers and carpenters. Second, he

DOG AND BONE 45

is very likely to become one of the 200,000 victims of DIY accidents recorded each year. In addition, all the evidence suggests that more than one-third of DIY projects are left unfinished, and professionals have to come in and clear up the mess, anyway.

But the "bodging" tradition goes back a long way. Jerome K. Jerome, in his 1889 comic novel *Three Men in a Boat,* describes the activities of his uncle Podger in putting up a picture, and the fear that he imposed in those around him. As the chaos continues:

> Aunt Maria would mildly observe that next time Uncle Podger was going to hammer a nail into the wall, she hoped he'd let her know in time so that she could make arrangements to go and spend a week with her mother.

Yet Uncle Podger's enthusiasm is never dimmed. As he steps back from his work around midnight and beholds the damage extending for yards around his crooked picture, he declares: "There you are.... Some people would have had a man in to do a little thing like that."

There is, of course, a painless alternative for filling your leisure time. Women, much smarter than men at most things, identified it a long time ago. It's safe, clean, not life-threatening at all, and all you need is a credit card. It's called retail therapy.

Dog and bone

You would never guess that this means a "phone." It's a well-known example of rhyming slang. This creative style of speech is a peculiarity of Cockneys, those born "within

hello?

the sound of Bow Bells," namely the bells of St. Mary-le-Bow Church in Cheapside in the city of London. They have a long renown as witty and enterprising street traders and, more recently, as financial market traders. These folk invented a way of substituting words for others that rhymed, calling "stairs," for example, "apples and pears." A hat is known as "a titfer" (short for "tit-for-tat").

The special feature of rhyming slang is that the rhyme comes from a pair of words, but only the first word is used as an abbreviation. So a phone ("dog and bone") is referred to as "a dog." A suit is a whistle (for "whistle and flute"). "Use your loaf!" means "Use your head (loaf of bread)." Put them together, and a hatless man on his way out might ask his trouble to be a dear and pop up the apples for his titfer.

See? It's easy when you know how!

Dog's life

Everyone knows that the English treat their dogs better than their children, and it is often noted that the Society for the Prevention of Cruelty to Animals was founded in England in 1824, 60 years before the National Society for the Prevention of Cruelty to Children. Is it deeply meaningful that the SPCA went on to become the *Royal Society* (RSPCA), while the children's society still waits for that honor?

What, then, lies behind this remarkable but apparently sincere attachment the English have to their dogs? Not to mention cats. The truth is, they seem more able to express themselves freely with animals than with other people. Anthropologist Kate Fox, who has dedicated her life to studying the strange ways of the English, ponders this aspect of their relationship with pets and explains convincingly: "Unlike our fellow Englishmen, animals are not embarrassed or put off by our un-English displays of emotion."

The word "dog" itself is peculiarly native to England and comes from an obscure Old English past. The alternative Germanic term "hound" refers mainly to hunting dogs, as in the phrase "to ride to hounds." In feudal society the best of such dogs might be given special treatment by their lordly master and be fed from his table. But lesser dogs out in the yard had a rougher time, and English is crammed with phrases that suggest a dog's life, at least up to the nineteenth century, truly was a miserable fate: dog-tired, dogsbody, going to the dogs, die like a dog,

ello?! ello?!!

and so on. For the most part, dogs invited contempt and cruelty. Even nowadays the question, "What was it like?" might produce the answer, "An absolute dog!" No positive qualities here, then.

But in curious contrast, the modern reality is that the English treat their dogs with huge affection, looking on them as fellows, close companions, and having a bond with them that lasts for life. The English adore the legendary image of a dog's faithfulness and, literally, "doggedness." Nature seems to provide plenty of evidence to justify this attitude. Endless anecdotes suggest that dogs are strangely and deeply attuned to their owners, with many observers believing their pets have psychic powers. The researcher and scientist Rupert Sheldrake, for example, has organized surveys to demonstrate that dogs (among other pets) waiting at home "know" the moment their owners leave the office and begin their homeward journey. If this is true, it leaves conventional scientific knowledge rather short on the facts.

So what is an English dog's life like these days? Some commentators think the sense of the phrase has gradually changed and that it now means to have a cosseted and comfortable existence, rather than the reverse. I am quite sure the Queen's corgi would agree with that. However, this cozy impression is not borne out by the evidence. According to a recent survey, the incidence of stray and abandoned dogs in England was around 90,000, an increase over the previous year.

What's going on here? Two extremes of behavior meeting in a confused national psyche? It does seem that, in their attitudes to animals and children, we find one of the paradoxes of the English temperament.

All the same, there is one common expression that continues to suggest that a bond between human and animal is more than mere friendship: "Love me, love my dog." Or rather, in practice: "Love my dog, love me." Observe dog owners meeting in a public park and you will see how it works. Better than a dating agency anytime.

Don't mind me!

One of the most nuanced phrases ever uttered, and very revealing of the apparently self-deprecating manners of an English person. Like **"Mmm," "Tell me about it,"** and **"With respect,"** the true meaning depends entirely on the context. But with such statements, very often the real sense is the opposite of what the words appear to mean. If you hear "Don't mind me!" then you are either listening to a genuine apology from someone for disturbing you or else being a complete nuisance yourself.

Similarly, "Tell me about it!" is usually uttered as an exclamation meaning, in reality: "I already know this so well, so don't even begin to tell me about it!" Like, "You can say that again!" it's certainly not an invitation to repeat what you just said.

Perhaps with phrases like these in mind, commonly used but often perplexing, the *2008 Rough Guide to England,* authored by four British travel writers, does warn overseas visitors that the English are "the most contradictory people imaginable" and comes to the slightly despairing conclusion that "However long you spend in the country, you'll never figure them out."

Doolally

Since it is not every day that you conquer an entire sub-continent, English military and cultural triumphs in India were crowned by Queen Victoria being declared Empress of India in 1877.

As a direct result of this bold move, the Queen's English went on to be enriched by some 70 years of Anglo-Indian expressions turned into colonial and military slang.

In case we think it was easy to govern a subcontinent with all its different races, languages, religions, and unfamiliar customs, there is plenty of evidence to suggest that the administrators and soldiers of the Raj were under a lot of mental pressure. One colorful expression that has survived is "to go doolally"; in other words, go a little bit crazy (also referred to in England as going round the bend). It comes from the name Deolali, a military camp 125 miles northeast of Bombay, where the British Army had an asylum for weary and demoralized troops. Soldiers often spent months there before being sent home to England, and when they arrived back in Old Blighty, it was obvious from their fragile state of mind that they had "gone to Deolali."

I have also heard, from those with old India connections, that the expression "to go round the bend" came from the same source, being the orientation of the railway line from Bombay to Nashik Road, the local station for Deolali. This is as good a theory as any and certainly beats the notion that Victorian mental hospitals had a bend in their driveways to distinguish them from stately homes. Crazy, indeed.

Eavesdropper

Before gutters and street drains were in common use, houses had wide eaves to allow rain to fall far from the walls and windows. This extended roof was known as the "eavesdrip" and, later, "eavesdrop." A passerby, standing under the eavesdrop, would be likely to hear conversations from within the house. Hence, "eaves-droppers" were those who listened in on private conversations. In the English code of behavior, this simply isn't done—except, of course, in the interests of national security.

Egghead

The label "egghead," used in both Britain and the United States, is a mildly disparaging term for an academic person. The English are, if anything, rather self-deprecating, at least on the surface. They also have a certain distrust of clever people (compare the loaded implication of the word "intellectual" in English with the admiring sense of *intellectuel* in

French). Note, too, the English criticism often used of a bright person: "Too clever for their own good."

A "boffin," in contrast, is a dedicated scientist who pays the price of exceptional intelligence through being rather eccentric. The classic portrait of Albert Einstein with his hair all over the place is a perfect illustration of a boffin. No one with so much hair could be an egghead, naturally.

Elbow grease

This phrase, meaning "hard physical work," goes back at least to the seventeenth century and refers in a joking way to the best method for polishing wood. A particularly English association lies in the old workshop tradition of playing tricks on new apprentices.

In printing workshops, one practice was to drop a tray of typefaces and then make the unfortunate youngster spend hours and hours putting them back in order. Many practical jokes were played on an apprentice's ignorance, and they included sending him to fetch some "elbow grease," a wild-goose chase in which the wretched boy would be sent all over until he either caught on to the joke or gave up.

Elevenses

The identification of a time of day with a snack seems logical enough. In England, elevenses are eaten at 11 o'clock in the morning and usually consist of a cup of tea or coffee and some sweet accompaniment in the form of cake or **biscuits**. One thing is clear: Without the solid food the occasion would only be tea or coffee and not elevenses.

Then it all starts to get mysterious. I can't find any explanation for why there are elevenses but no oneses, fourses, or sixes. There may be a connection with the eating habits of the English in the Indian Raj, when elevenses presented an opportunity for an early apéritif (plus, of course, the obligatory cake or biscuits) with tif-fin, or light lunch, beginning at 1 o'clock.

English rose

This is a winsome description of a kind of English feminine beauty, characterized by a delicate skin of shades of white and pink. Heroines of romantic novels of a certain period would certainly be English roses. In 1997 Elton John wrote "Good-bye England's Rose" to memorialize Princess Diana after her tragic death. Now, 14 years later, the British are thrilled to have a new English rose. No longer dubbed "Katie Waitie," Kate Middleton's marriage to Prince William, the future King of England, has British fashionis-tas hankering after her to be the next Royal style icon.

Although Kate is referred to constantly by British newspapers as having English rose looks because of her natural beauty, the English rose was originally an emblem that signified the uniting of the House of York and House of Lancaster after the War of the Roses, which was a series of conflicts fought for many years between these Houses. The emblem of the House of York was the white rose. Lancaster adopted a red rose to distinguish them from their opponents. When Henry Tudor emerged victorious from the wars, the Tudor period began. He married the daughter of the Duke of York and created a new emblem, combining the red rose of Lancaster with the white rose of York, thus creating the English rose.

'Er indoors

Phrases that catch on and become popular tend to reveal something about the attitudes and sense of humor of the English. For example, "'Er indoors" is a phrase from the 1980s TV comedy series *Minder* and used by Arthur Daley to refer to his wife—a character who is never seen. Arthur is a wheeler-dealer who mixes so much in shady business that he has to hire a "minder," London slang for bodyguard.

John Mortimer's lawyer character in the series *Rumpole of the Bailey* also has a strong-minded wife, Hilda, whom he refers to discreetly as "She who must be obeyed."

A few other English TV catchphrases have lodged in day-to-day speech in recent years:

I've started, so I'll finish. The frequent cry of Magnus Magnusson chairing the quiz program *Mastermind* when a bell indicated the end of the permitted time for a contestant.

Didn't he/she do well! The phrase often used by Bruce Forsyth, host of *The Generation Game*.

Don't mention the war! The warning from Basil Fawlty, a neurotic hotel owner, to his staff about the presence of German guests in the hotel, in *Fawlty Towers*.

Am I bovvered? The cry of Catherine Tate, playing the teenage character Lauren, indicating she isn't "bothered"—that is, doesn't really care about much at all.

Fair play

Shakespeare used both the phrases "fair play" and "foul play" in his works and may well have coined both, thus giving us some principles for behavior that have become legendary in the English character. Whatever precisely Shakespeare meant by them—his sense may have been closer to the idea of mere civilized observance and its opposite—nowadays we interpret the phrase "fair play" as sportsmanship, playing by the rules with a certain nobility of spirit.

There may well be a leftover of chivalric courtesy in the term, implying that there are underhand or ignoble deeds or actions that a "gentleman" simply doesn't engage in. Children of a certain period learned these rules at school and, equally, through the rules of the playground. In childhood fights, you didn't attack someone from behind, when they were on the ground, or gang up two against one. These were all unwritten rules that were honored as much as the written rules of team games.

It is depressing now, against the background of that tradition, to see highly paid soccer players tripping from behind, grabbing shirts, and elbowing—in a jungle atmosphere where almost everything goes—in the pathetic hope that no one will notice. There was a time, I seem to remember, when the "beautiful game" really was more beautiful, when players respected the spirit, the character, and the image of the game, and understood far more than we see now, the real meaning of "fair play."

Feather in your cap

It would be a pity not to include at least one reference to England's chivalric past. While "a feather in your cap" is now used generally as meaning a token of achievement, it refers to the fact that, in medieval times, knights were honored for their bravery in the field with plumes to wear on their helmets, often symbolic of the defeated enemy. The best-known example of this has to be the Prince of Wales's Feathers, the three ostrich feathers bestowed on the Black Prince after the Battle of Crécy in 1346, and now the principal emblem of the badge of the heir to the throne. The three feathers can be seen on the current two-pence coin in Britain.

Feathers continue to have a symbolic value in heraldry; only those with certain office or honors have the privilege of wearing them. A number of inns and pubs also bear the name The Feathers, in recognition of the royal coat of arms.

First cuckoo

There is a persistent myth that an annual event occurs in the Letters to the Editor column of *The Times* when someone writes to announce the date at the start of the summer migration when they hear "the first cuckoo."

The Times has gone to some trouble, however, to publish the fact that they do not print readers' letters on this subject. "According to our digital archive we haven't actually published a straightforward 'first cuckoo' letter since 1940," they claim.

Even when this tradition was at its height, it seems that doubts entered the journalistic mind, especially following letters to the editor such as that from a Mr. Fydekker, dated February 12, 1913:

> Sir, I regret to say that, in common with many other persons, I have been completely deceived in the matter of the supposed cuckoo of February 4. The note was uttered by a bricklayer's labourer at work on a house.... I have interviewed the man, who tells me that he is able to draw cuckoos from considerable distances by the exactness of his imitation of their notes....

Flummox

A dialectal term, first recorded in the nineteenth century, meaning to puzzle or confuse. No one knows where this word comes from, not even the *Oxford English Dictionary*. But we can imagine it on the lips of a countryman in some rural English setting, staring at the horizon as he tries to figure out the meaning to some deep question and eventually comes out with "Well, that's got me right flummoxed!"

Flutter

This is a lovely old word with a venerable history, meaning to float gently up and down on the waves, or to move in the air. Nowadays its popular sense of "to have a small bet" comes from that charming English tradition that allows them to have a certain number of little vices without guilt.

Betting and gambling are, of course, social evils, and the Protestant streak in English life, dating from the Reformation, certainly does not approve of that. However, the whole nation can guiltlessly assemble each spring at the Grand National, the most exciting horse race of the year, and have a "flutter." I like the word's suggestion of a slightly racing heartbeat, which expresses so nicely the amateurish pleasure of the whole moment. It is believed that the Queen herself, a keen race-goer as well as owner, has a little flutter on the side. And if she doesn't, her mother in her time certainly did.

Flyover

This has nothing to do with the way the British drive, although it's known we do fly down the A40. A flyover is simply a bridge that takes one road above another road. The same as an overpass would be in America.

Gazump

Usually so proud of their reputation for playing fair, the English have a curious blind spot when it comes to buying and selling houses. To "gazump" is to raise the price of a piece of real estate after the sale has been agreed to but before the contract is signed, usually on the pretext that the owner has received a higher offer elsewhere. The original buyer is then forced to raise his offer, or the property goes to the higher bidder.

This unethical but not illegal practice appeared first with the spelling "gazoomph" and was derived from an older and more general term "gazumph" (or gezump) for the various kinds of swindling that go on at dishonest auctions.

Gobsmacked

This wonderful term comes from joining two delightfully incorrect slang words: "gob," a not very polite slang word for mouth, of Celtic origin; and "smacked," as we find in a related phrase, "smacked in the kisser." But no violence is intended in "gobsmacked," which means "left speechless"—though this may have the same effect as being smacked in the kisser.

Gobsmacked cgained notoriety from Conservative politician Chris Patten, a member of Mrs. Thatcher's administration, who liked to descend from the heights of his classical education and speak the language of the people. "Double whammy" (double blow) and "porkies" (= pork pies = lies, in rhyming slang) were other colorful terms he used. Whether because of, or in spite of, the irritation caused by such talk, he lost his parliamentary seat in the 1992 election and went off to annoy the Chinese as the last governor of Hong Kong.

Gone for a Burton

Beer and the military have a long and happy association that goes back many centuries in England. A common euphemism used in the Second World War, especially with RAF pilots, was the phrase "gone for a Burton," referring to fellow airmen who were killed or went missing. Burton, here, refers to a well-known beer that originated in the Midlands town of Burton-on-Trent.

Though no one can actually pin down the origin of this phrase, I like the theory that it came from a series of beer advertisements in the interwar years that showed a picture of a sports team with a gap where one member is missing, with the caption GONE FOR A BURTON. The Burton Brewery itself was no longer operating under that name in the 1940s, but the Burton style of strong dark beer was still widely enjoyed and would certainly have been known in air force bars around the country.

"Gone west" is another phrase associated with war. Put briefly, to go west is "to die." We find it in use by both soldiers and airmen during the First World War, to describe being sent back from the trenches, thus sent westward, usually with fatal injuries, as minor wounds were treated in the battle area. But the concept has much older associations in ancient spirituality. Because the sun went down over the western ocean, there was the tradition, both in Christian and pagan European thought, that the soul's journey to its ultimate end lay "westward."

Googly

The English language is full of phrases borrowed from cricket, such as "keep a straight bat" or "be completely stumped," or "on a sticky wicket." Often these have some moral or philosophical edge to them, associated with the traditionally upright image of the game. "It isn't cricket!" was once how a certain brand of Englishman protested against a less-than-honorable action.

Probably, a good deal of this noble moralizing has been lost with the state of the modern game. One nice term that survives in general use and defies translation is the "googly," a certain throw of the ball so that it lands in one direction and then bounces in another, thus confusing the batsman. The word now means any tricky challenge presented to an opponent or competitor. "I bowled him a real googly," one might say with delight

Ha-ha

This odd noun, meaning a kind of wall, is quintessentially English and tells us a lot about ourselves. "Ha-ha" is the English onomatopoeic word for laughter, and the name arises from the humorous reaction of people when they first see a ha-ha wall. But what's funny about a wall?

It all has to do with the English and their love-hate relationship with nature. As with their attitude to animals and children, the English response to nature is sort of confused: They spend an equal amount of time walking over it as they do building over it. To the modern suburban gardener, nature is the enemy (see "Pottering"), but more widely, this has not always been the case. If we go back to the seventeenth and eighteenth centuries, we find the earliest signs of what was to become the Romantic movement, reasserting humankind's closeness to nature as a source of beauty, feeling, and inspiration. Usually this is taken to be a reaction to the cerebral rationalism of the Enlightenment. But the English were never quite so persuaded as the French, for instance, that reason was the beginning and end of everything.

The English, as with most important matters, retained an amateurish approach, especially in the activity of thinking. This allowed them to dabble and remain slightly out of control in philosophical issues. And in their gardens, too. While the French created Versailles, with its clipped hedges and symmetrical patterns, the English created undulating parks that took nature as it was and just...well, reorganized it slightly. Marie Antoinette so liked this idea (she had problems adapting to stuffy old Versailles, anyway) that she created her own *jardin anglais,* a secret place where all the French rules were broken, and plants and trees were allowed, within limits, to be themselves.

Now we come to the ha-ha. So devoted were the English to their rolling and natural estates, that they got the notion they would like to sit in their homes and see it all unfurl before them. But traditional walls got in the way and cut them off. Hence, someone had the bright idea of bordering the home garden with a sunken wall, keeping out the livestock and the deer while allowing an open and uninterrupted view. An invisible wall. No wonder people exclaimed "Ha-ha!" when they first saw it.

Hair of the dog (that bit you)

Across the Queen's green and pleasant land on any Sunday morning, you can be sure that a good number of her loyal subjects are nursing a fierce headache after one beer or two too many the previous evening.

English folk wisdom dictates that a shot of the drink that got you into this state—a hair of the dog that bit you—will supposedly clear your head in no time.

The phrase is thought to come from the ancient medical principle and practice of "like cures like," according to which a dog bite would be healed by rubbing it with a burnt hair of the offending dog.

Handsome

Note that when used to describe a man, "handsome" is a hugely positive word, indicative of his strong, attractive, masculine features. When used of a woman, the word is still a compliment, but one soured slightly by a subtle connotation of these manly qualities.

A handsome woman is one who is attractive in a way that is striking and imposing rather than conventionally pretty.

How's your father?

Yet another slang expression for sexual activity, this is a twentieth-century phrase, probably originating with the music-hall comedian Harry Tate (1872–1940), who would use it to change the subject whenever a conversation took a difficult turn. From this, it came into general use for anything a speaker did not wish to name, and then, inevitably, as sex was so often the unnamed subject, it found its home in expressions like "having a bit of how's-your-father" (*see also* "It").

In a spoof etymology the phrase comes from the practice of Victorian fathers hiding under their daughters' voluminous skirts so that a panting suitor would always carefully ask: "How's your father?" before lurching into the arms of his beloved.

Humbug!

Humbug has come to be associated with the most famous unlikeable hero of all time, Charles Dickens's Ebenezer Scrooge, in *A Christmas Carol*.

We know that Scrooge hated Christmas and thought it a waste of time, not to mention money. He despised the merriment around him and was disinclined even to let his poor overworked clerk, Bob Cratchit, have Christmas Day at home with his family. To every suggestion of generosity, bonhomie, or kindness, Scrooge's scowling riposte was "Bah! Humbug!" But then, through some kind of miraculous intervention involving the ghosts of Christmas past, present, and future, he underwent a conversion and became a reconstructed bourgeois—sensitive, kind, and unable to pass a poor man in the street without offering to help him.

I'm a Dutchman

Partly because of the Englishman's insular character and also due to their history of roaming the world aggressively, the English have a rich store of abuse in their language for foreigners—mostly directed toward other Europeans who, at various times, have competed with them for power. It is hard to imagine now, but the Dutch were once the special object of English abuse and contempt, probably because Dutch seafaring skills were equal to theirs. Indeed, the English borrowed a wide range of sailing words from the Dutch language, including skipper, landlubber, boom, hull, sloop, and a whole lot more.

During the Anglo-Dutch wars of the seventeenth century, in 1667, a Dutch fleet sailed up the Medway river and did much damage to English ships and defenses, as well as towing away a flagship. A wave of anti-Dutch feeling swept over London, and pamphlets and newspapers all had their day ridiculing the Netherlandish people as "a nation of cheese-mongers and herring-picklers, muddy and greedy," according to Henry Hitchings, author of *Defining the World*. This animosity is illustrated with the many negative terms that still survive today when it comes to the Dutch. Terms like "bumpkin" and "nitwit" were used to describe their national character. Expressions like Dutch courage, Dutch auction, and similar phrases played on the notion of insincerity and falsehood; then the ultimate insult of all, in statements like "These pies are the best in town, and if you find better, then I'm a Dutchman."

Much ill feeling between the two nations was finally laid to rest in 1688 when William of Orange, Protestant nephew of Charles II and James II, landed in England to assume the throne, prevent another English Civil War, and form an alliance that would contain the rising French influence under the Sun King, Louis XIV.

In a nutshell

"Oh God, I could be bounded in a nutshell and count myself a King of infinite space . . ." cries Hamlet in Shakespeare's famous tragic play. But the meaning of the expression—to put a lot into a small space—goes way back to classical times, to Pliny's *Natural History,* in which he wrote: "Cicero records that a parchment copy of Homer's poem *The Iliad* was enclosed in a nutshell (*in nuce*)."

In Shakespeare's own time, there was a version of a Bible created that was considered small enough to fit into a nutshell, and that curiosity may have come to the playwright's notice.

In a pretty pickle

Another phrase found in Shakespeare, this time on the lips of Trinculo in Shakespeare's *The Tempest*: "I have been in such a pickle since I saw you last."

The phrase was already in existence, borrowed from the Dutch expression "to sit in a pickle"—pickle being the salt brine used for preserving meat or fish, really not a very pleasant place to be. With time a nice English ironic twist to the phrase became "in a pretty pickle," thus typically understating the experience of being in an unpleasant, embarrassing, or awkward situation.

"To be in a stew" is another common food metaphor, here with the meaning of being in trouble or rage over a bad situation.

Either of these sounds like an undesirable place to be getting hot under the collar.

It

Of course, nobody knows what "it" is, but that's the whole point. The English, in their amusingly bashful way, will only ever refer to sex indirectly. Hence, we see, often as stickers in the back window of cars, CLIMBERS DO IT ON MOUNTAINS or CAMPERS DO IT IN TENTS. The variations are endlessly creative. Such innuendo is a staple ingredient of English humor, and it goes back all the way to Chaucer and Shakespeare.

Humphrey Lyttelton, erstwhile presenter of a popular English radio show called "I'm Sorry, I Haven't a Clue," invented an imaginary assistant called Samantha and opened the show every week with some scandalously ambiguous comment. The following example plays on the similarity in sound between "tenor" (male singer) and "tenner" (common term for a 10-pound note): "Samantha once trained opera singers—having seen what she did to the baritone, the director is keen to see what she might do for a tenor."

The special quality of innuendo, of course, is to make the statement in all innocence so the device is frequently used where children can happily take one meaning while adults will see the sexual reference. Balloons, jugs, melons, buns, beaver, muff, poker, tool, staff, snake, sword—all these can figure in English innuendo as indirect references to parts of the body. The whole sense and enjoyment are in the ambiguity of interpretation. In a classic example of this, academics are still arguing over whether or not Shakespeare's Sonnet 52, written for his beloved young lord, is pure sexual innuendo from beginning to end: "So am I as the rich, whose blessed key/Can bring him to his sweet up-locked treasure."

Nowadays there is a tendency in film and drama production to make Shakespeare's sexual references more explicit, which may reflect how his lines were played in his own time. This is a sign of modern times and tastes, but in the case of Jane Austen and more modest classical authors, this can result in a loss of the subtlety and wit of the original.

Jingoism

This term, referring to aggressive and overconfident nationalism, takes us back to the days of the Empire, when Britain ruled the waves and a lot more besides. In the 1870s Russia, a long-standing threat to British interests throughout the nineteenth century, moved into the Balkans in an expansionist gesture against Turkey, wildly upsetting Britain. As a result, the major European powers summoned both sides to the Congress of Berlin in 1878 and worked out a settlement, as the diplomats say, to restore stability. What this really means, of course, is that they carved up the world to suit oneself and one's allies, in this case the Austro-Hungarian dynasty of the Hapsburgs, who were terrified of Slavic nationalism rearing its head.

A popular song had already raised British spirits at home, and a phrase in its chorus became a byword for imperialistic gloating over the upcoming challenge to Russia:

We don't want to fight, but by Jingo if we do
We've got the ships, we've got the men, we've got the
money too.
We've fought the Bear before, and while we're Britons true
The Russians shall not have Constantinople.

Up to this time, "by Jingo" was no more than one of the many euphemisms for "by God" or "by Jesus" in popular language, but now it found its new form of "jingoes," or warmongers, in a letter from the campaigning socialist G. J. Holyoake to the radical London newspaper, the *Daily News*.

Jumble sale

Jumble is a curious little word that has done a lot of traveling in its time, starting out as a verb meaning something like *stumble* or *tumble,* then denoting sexual activity, as tumble still does. However, it reinvented itself as a noun in the seventeenth century, meaning a "confused mixture," which is how we find it in Samuel Johnson's *Dictionary of 1755,* with the added sense of "violent or confused agitation."

All this takes us to the wonderful tradition of the jumble sale, a confused mixture of items all donated by members of a church or community, as a way of fund-raising. The jumble sale is where the English spirit of optimism reigns supreme, always hoping to turn up some precious antique among the pile of discarded items cleared from the attic after years of neglect. And it does happen, too, from time to time! The Americans do the same, right in their own driveway.

Killing's the matter!

"Killing's the matter!" exclaims Mrs. Malaprop, a character in Richard Sheridan's 1775 play *The Rivals*. "But he can tell you the perpendiculars." By which, of course, she meant the "particulars."

Mrs. Malaprop has given her name to malapropisms, a classic kind of linguistic error explored and condemned in *The King's English* (see "King's English"). It arises from trying to sound educated by using a long word but mistakenly substituting another that sounds like the one you really want. There are hilarious malapropisms from all over the world (some are also known as Bushisms), but some of the funniest come from the mouth of Mrs. Malaprop herself. Here is an example, followed by the words she really meant to say:

"She's as headstrong as an allegory on the banks of the Nile." (alligator)

"I am sorry to say, Sir Anthony, that my affluence over my niece is very small." (influence)

"Oh! it gives me the hydrostatics to such a degree." (hysterics)

"He is the very pineapple of politeness!" (pinnacle)

"I have since laid Sir Anthony's preposition before her." (proposition)

(The) King's English

As *The King's Speech,* crowned Best Picture at the 2011 Oscars, pointedly conveys, communication from the monarchy is of huge importance to the English people. And unfortunately for King George VI, this expectation forced him to overcome a debilitating stutter in order to address the nation during World War II, having been thrown into the limelight after his brother Edward abdicated the throne three years earlier.

The King's English, written by H. W. and F. G. Fowler and first published in 1906, has made no less of an impact on the English. It is a classic description and robust defense of their language as it should be, according to the rules of grammar and good style. With its stern commentaries on everything from unattached participles to "trite phrases" and "cheap originality," it has been a standard reference work ever since, cited whenever ammunition is needed to ridicule any writer's grammatical blunder or inelegance.

The diehard approach to such matters has softened considerably in recent times, as linguists have come to find positive virtues in English "as she is spoke," rather than constrained by the rulebook. So it is with whimsical interest, rather than mischievous intent, that we look at its section on Americanisms, which opens thus:

Americanisms are foreign words, and should be so treated. To say this is not to insult the American language.... It must be recognised that they and we, in parting some hundreds of years ago, started on slightly divergent roads in language long before we did so in politics.

The Fowler brothers' severe conclusion is that "The English and the American language and literature are both good things, but they are better apart than mixed."

Kiss me, Hardy

Much discussion has been generated throughout the years over this odd little phrase, which was supposed to be the last utterance of English national hero Lord Nelson to Captain Thomas Hardy. Nelson was mortally wounded by a musket ball in the final hours of the Battle of Trafalgar when, in one of the most decisive engagements of the Napoleonic wars, the English fleet defeated the Spanish and French naval force off the southwest coast of Spain.

Some, determined that Nelson would never have said anything so **soppy** to another man, argued that he really said, "Kismet, Hardy," referring to fate or destiny. However, accounts given by eyewitnesses do confirm that Hardy kissed him, a quite normal and unambiguous gesture of friendship between men at the time.

Knackered

This term is used not only as an adjective to describe someone who is extremely tired or something that is worn out because of overuse, such as a handbag, but it also functions as a noun and a verb. For instance, it can mean to severely damage: "I knackered my leg playing rugby."

As a noun, a knacker is someone who buys worn-out or old livestock in order to sell the hides or the meat as dog food. After the breakout of mad cow disease in the 1980s, the phrase "ready for the knacker's yard" gained great notoriety. A knacker is also someone who buys structures and takes them apart to sell off the individual pieces. Same concept; different source.

Knuckle down

Knuckling down strikes me as a very English characteristic, in the sense of accepting difficulties that arise and just getting on with things. It is all the more surprising that its origin is the humble game of marbles and comes from the rule that you must keep your knuckle down where your marble has just been. So from "obey the rule," knuckle down had the eighteenth-century dictionary sense of "to stoop, bend, yield, comply with, or submit to."

Of course, the unspoken rule in English behavior is to accept without complaint, so they have made this a positive virtue—to apply oneself to the task as needed. This is very different from "knuckle under," which now has acquired the original meaning of "submit" but comes from American usage.

Lager

When most people think of lager, they think of color. Lagers range from very pale to deep black and represent the vast majority of beers produced. But really, the term lager means storage, and lagering refers to the brewing techniques that make this popular beer.

Beer that's been fermented at a cool temperature, around 50°F (10°C), then stored for 30 days or longer close to the freezing point, is called lager. Good lager depends on a slow-acting yeast that ferments at a low temperature when stored. Lager, as opposed to ale, ferments in the bottle, which gives natural carbonation.

Lager brewing in Britain began with the Austro Bavarian Lager Beer Company of Tottenham, North London, which was being brewed by an entirely German staff in 1882. By 1976 one in four pints sold was lager, but today things have changed dramatically. Now lager is taking a backseat to ale, which is rivaling wine as the British drink of sophistication (*see also* "Pint of Bitter").

Lame duck

Why duck, and why lame? No one really knows, but
this graphic expression is as common these days in the
United States as in the U.K. to describe a politician who
is still in office but unable, either constitutionally or
through waning power, to exercise his functions.

However, the phrase was not originally political but
comes from a financial background. As far back as the eighteenth century, it was used in the London Stock Market to
refer to an investor or broker unable to pay up on settlement
day. Bulls, bears, and lame ducks are all financial market
metaphors of that period that still survive today.

Lift

The American version of the elevator. The British claim
to know lift etiquette—that is, no talking while in transit
and, of course, no singing or whistling. But did you know
that if passengers board while conversing, you should
never join in unless invited? Or that you should never
make fun of people when they get off the elevator because
other passengers still in the lift may know the person?

If you are not aware of these simple rules of lift etiquette, there are websites that can help you. That way,
you'll be sure never to push the emergency stop button
to have a private moment with your partner.

Load of cobblers

Another of these elusive phrases with their origin in
rhyming slang, but I would guess that in this very popu-

lar saying, most people don't actually know the key word. "A load of cobbler's awls" is the full phrase, in this case "awls" to rhyme with "balls," which probably needs no further explanation.

Local pub

At the very center of English village life, the local pub is traditionally not only a social club, it is a haven for the lonely and weary, a welcome refuge for the traveler, and an intelligence center for all that is going on in the village. As England's major cities sprang up, the tradition of the "local" transferred to urban life as well, where large conurbations often swallowed up older towns and villages, which to some extent kept their local character.

The lounge bar, the public bar, and the snug are different areas of a traditional pub, dating from earlier times. When workmen on their way home from their trades and labors wanted to pop in to their "local" in their working clothes, they went to the public bar—a "spit-and-sawdust" area where the furniture was bare wood and the floor uncarpeted. Those wanting a more genteel evening out went to the lounge bar, where they paid a little extra for their drinks to have cushioned seats or benches, carpet on the floor, and a supposedly higher standard of decor. The snug was a tiny space, often between the two bars, where a couple could have a little privacy.

Traditionally, English drinking hours are strictly controlled. Around 11:00 P.M. the landlord rings a bell and gives his customers 10 minutes' "drinking-up time" to down their drinks and leave the premises in an orderly fashion. In remoter places, there survives the discreet tradition of the "lock-in," where a select group of the landlord's regulars are allowed to stay on and drink once the doors are shut and the curtains drawn. The 2005 relaxation of licensing hours was supposed to have ended this practice, but it was so illicit that it most likely continues.

However, pubs seem to be in trouble. The British Beer and Pub Association claims pub beer sales are at half the level they were in 1979. And—according to CAMRA (the Campaign for Real Ale)—pubs are closing at the rate of 60 a month (*see also* "lager"). Country pubs seem the hardest hit, with the recent ban on smoking and severe penalties for drunk driving making people more inclined to drink at home. For many pubs, survival depends on encouraging families to eat out: One pub chain recently claimed that food sales account for 37 percent of their turnover, compared with beer at 31 percent. The onus seems to be on publicans, then, to work at improving their food and at losing the terrible label that the overpriced, poor-quality "pub grub" has acquired over the years.

Alternatively, with so many small village shops and post offices closing around the country, the suggestion has come from no less than Prince Charles, heir to the throne, that country pubs, in a new initiative for survival, could combine all these roles into one. Such a change could alter the perception of the "local" in a big way.

Lollipop man/lady

This is the common name for what is officially called the School Crossing Patrol Service, set up in the 1950s to assist young children to cross the road on the way to or from school. First established by the police and maintained later by local councils, the patrols have legal powers under the Road Traffic Act 1984, and car drivers have the legal duty to respect the patrol and to stop when required.

The patrolmen or women carry a large round Stop sign that looks like a lollipop—hence, the popular name. Many children grow up with good memories of the cheery smile of the lollipop man or lady helping them cross the street, an image of security and safety. The very term "lollipop" is a positive one for children, as lollipops are considered to be special treats.

But all is not well in lollipop land. There are increasing instances of intimidation and aggression from members of the public, and in 2007 over 1,400 patrols were assaulted, with many victims needing hospital treatment. It appears that drivers and others nowadays resent the demand to stop—a depressing symptom of the impatience and haste of modern life.

Loo

This is a middle- to upper-class euphemism for lavatory. It derives from "Waterloo," but the only association known between the Battle of Waterloo (1815) and lavatories stems from the Duke of Wellington's being asked by a young officer's mother what advice he could give her son starting on a military career. The duke is supposed to have uttered the unforgettable reply: "Never miss an opportunity to pass water."

Lorry

The British word for truck, although lorry drivers are being referred to more and more as truckers. But while some are dismayed that the American term is overtaking tradition, some investigation into the subject has found that the word "truck" actually goes all the way back to ancient Greece, from the Latin word *trochus,* meaning wheel. The British term didn't appear until 300 years later from the verb "lurry," which means to tug or pull.

Whatever you choose to call them, these drivers seem to be all over the road, which is all right, as long as they're not in the fast lane. But you may see a decline in lorries soon. To green transport, the European Parliament is trying to pass legislation to make lorry drivers pay for noise and air pollution caused by their vehicles. They believe doing this will force companies to forego lorries and instead put their freight on railroads and ships. The new rules would apply to any motorway in the EU.

Mad as a March hare

Hares are beautiful, elegant creatures, but when it comes to breeding season, they indulge in eccentric and wild behavior. They appear to have boxing matches with one another, jump in the air, and do other odd antics, giving the impression of a degree of madness. The expression "mad as a March hare" goes back hundreds of years and is found in Chaucer's "Friar's Tale" in the fourteenth century.

Both hares and hatmakers (hatters) were associated with madness, the latter supposedly suffering because of the poisoning effect of the mercury they used in their craft. In one of the most hilarious scenes in children's literature, Lewis Carroll's Alice comes across both the March Hare and the Mad Hatter having a tea party with a dormouse, which they end up shoving into a teapot.

Maiden aunt

For sociological reasons that are hard to pin down, middle-class English families often have an unmarried, or maiden, aunt. These ladies are formidable members of society who use their energy in many public-spirited ways and are usually committed "churchgoers." They dress in robust, sensible clothing, tweed skirts and flat shoes preferred, with steely hairdos and a brisk manner that comes across as rather severe. Embracing children is not something they usually do.

In a famous speech a few years ago, the then prime minister John Major (a great lover of cricket) was reported as saying: "Fifty years on from now, Britain [that is, England] will still be the country of long shadows on county [cricket] grounds, warm beer, invincible green suburbs, dog lovers, and old maids bicycling to Holy Communion through the morning mist." The original description came from the work of the novelist and essayist George Orwell, an enthusiast for all things English and traditional.

Manor

The English language owes a huge debt to the French, in particular to the Norman conquerors of the eleventh century, who in one fell swoop brought it veal, pork, beef, mutton, venison, castles, domains, and last but not least, manors. The references to meat, by the way, come from the fact that these are the French-derived terms for the food served at the table to England's foreign overlords. Meanwhile, English-speaking serfs and peasants continued to raise pigs, cows, goats, and sheep.

Manor, meaning the residence or principal house on an estate, comes directly from the French *manoir,* in its turn from the Latin *manere,* which means to stay. The feudal pattern, working like a pyramid from the poorest at the bottom up through various degrees of privilege to the ruler at the very top, was all based on land ownership and the income it provided. At a local level the tenure of land was granted to the "lord of the manor," or *seigneur,* whose tenants actually worked the fields. This simple arrangement, enshrined in the *Domesday Book,* was to establish the character of rural England for centuries to follow. Even now, families exist that have manorial rights going back hundreds of years, and manors continue to be bought and sold, along with their titles.

Borrowing from this strong sense of ownership, the Londoner talks of his or her manor—namely, their corner or village in the metropolis.

Meat and potatoes

A heartwarming and enjoyable expression, full of nourishment and with a sturdy reality to it. To be a meat-and-potatoes man is to be one who is not concerned with frills and fancies, just a straightforward kind of guy. Meanwhile, the meat and potatoes of a book, or a text, or an agreement are the basic and most fundamental part.

This phrase appears to date from the middle of the twentieth century and may convey something of the postwar shortages in Britain at a time when meat was still rationed and when a proper meal was considered to be made up of both protein and carbohydrates. Other, rugby team–style meanings have been suggested for this expression, which I cannot possibly begin to explore, this being a decent family book.

Middle England

A phrase often on the lips of politicians and pollsters, by which they mean the middle part of England, which is at the center of the voting spectrum.

Middle England, it has been said, has its spiritual home in Tunbridge Wells, a town in Kent that is carefully conservative in its outlook. When you think of Tunbridge Wells, "what comes to mind?" asked the BBC (April 13, 1999). "Doilies, Women's Institute, semidetached, cricket on the green, retired colonels, bone china, bridge evenings, perhaps?" In other words, all the accoutrements of a past and more genteel age, redolent with Georgian and Victorian elegance and well-being. "It stands for everything that made Britain great, before the ghastly dawn of unemployment, drug abuse, foul-mouthed, disrespectful youth and teenage single mothers." Well, **Disgusted (of Tunbridge Wells)** would certainly agree with that.

Mind your p's and q's

A gentle admonition, usually to children, to mind their manners, perhaps as they are about to go to tea with a **maiden aunt**. There are a dozen suggestions for the derivation of this saying, ranging from the instructions of a French dancing master to mind your feet and wigs (*pieds et queues*) to advice for apprentice printers not to mix up metal type, a tavern keeper's traditional method of chalking up "pints and quarts" drunk by their clients, or quite simply a shortened corruption of "pleases and thank–yous."

Everyone has his or her favorite explanation, mine being the printer's guard against confusion over the similar and reversible shape of p's and q's. Some have argued that these letters are not even as common as b's and d's, which are also reversible and could easily be substituted in the phrase. But this misses the whole point that, in the font tray, p's and q's are actually side by side.

Mmm

Those familiar with English conversation will recognize this common reply to a question, while feeling that its meaning is never quite clear. This is because it can actually have one or even two of several meanings, depending on intonation and gesture (which may be just a movement of the eyebrows). It can mean *Yes, No, Maybe, Rather not, Don't think so, Sometimes, Oh, yes? Really?* or *What do you mean?*

A shake or nod of the head will sometimes tell you if the general meaning is positive or negative. The longer Mmm, as in Mmmmmm, can be taken as indicating severe doubt or reservation (*see also* "Umming and erring").

Mockney

One of the supposed revolutions in modern English
life has been the so-called "social leveling" of the classes,
a development that arose from the political principle of
equal opportunity for all. This is such a radical notion
that they had to learn it from their breakaway American
colony rather than find out for themselves. But it does
seem that they are making their way there slowly.

One sign of the times is a kind of reverse snobbery
that makes it unfashionable to be upper class, and trendy
to have what Rudyard Kipling called "the common
touch." Although a generation ago young people shed
their regional accents in order to get on in the world,
now they deliberately hide their "received pronunciation" (sometimes called BBC English) and put on an east
London, county of Essex, style of speech, more associated
with street traders than with aristocratic halls.

Phonetics experts will tell you more about this, but
a key feature of this stylized pronunciation is the glot-
tal stop, involving an arrested breath at the back of the
palate instead of a completely enunciated voiceless pre-
palatal occlusive. You get the idea. Such "mockney"—or
mock Cockney—is seen as a way of mingling with people of all classes without appearing threateningly superior
with your accent. Even the Queen herself has been persuaded to join in (see "Queen's speech").

Muck/mucky

For people doing serious things with the land, whether
farming or mining, muck is a serious word. Farmers

spread it; miners pile it high. Equally, nothing could be more serious than the classic image of the feet-on-the-ground Yorkshire businessman uttering the phrase "Where there's muck, there's brass." This is not a new idea or even an exclusively northern one, as shown by the English proverb "Muck and money go together"—a saying that goes back at least 300 years.

In the English world at large, though, muck has no value; in fact, it is just the opposite. Muck is basically dirt and nothing else. In the past the form *muck-a-muck* or *muckety-muck* was used as a taunting name for someone of airs and self-importance, perhaps because the appealingly blunt sound of the word could bring anyone down a peg. It is a four-letter word, after all, with kinship to the Old Norse term *myki*, meaning "dung." From dirt in a physical sense, it has also come to mean "filth"—that is, morally dubious entertainment.

Muck and mucky appear in many different sayings, (*muck about, muck in, muck around, muck up*) as well as songs and phrases. Though widely used throughout England, the words continue to have a northern ring about them. Take, for example, Stan Kelly's 1960s song "The Liverpool Lullaby," recorded in an inimitable accent by Cilla Black:

> *Oh you are a mucky kid,*
> *Dirty as a dustbin lid.*
> *When he hears the things you did,*
> *You'll gerra belt from your Dad.*

Naff

It is hard to imagine that a prime minister's briefs could become the focus of national attention, but that was the misfortune that befell John Major soon after his arrival on Downing Street in 1990. A TV news image of his clothes in slight disarray revealed that he wore his shirt *inside* his briefs instead of tucked between his briefs and his pants. One needs to have attended a boys boarding school to appreciate the vital difference between these two arrangements. One is fine and acceptable; the other is incredibly but laughably "naff."

Boys will be boys, and for years afterward political commentators and cartoonists mercilessly scorned Major's naffness, depicting him as Superuselessman, with jockey shorts worn over his pants, in the style of Superman's red briefs. "He's still a joke," wrote the cartoonist Steve Bell years later in 2002, thus proving that naffness is something that is never lived down, no matter how high you rise in public life or how many decades pass.

Nappy

Although the English do like to take a rest once in a while in the afternoon, this is not what it means. A nappy is a diaper, and it originated from the word napkin. And there are lots of other "baby" words the English use that will leave a new mother from somewhere else at a complete loss. For instance, a cot is a crib, a pushchair a stroller, and a pram ... well, that's a large stroller in which the top lifts off the wheels to become a cot—a crib—and then it would be called a carry cot.... In other words, it's short for perambulator.

The one thing the English do have in common with Americans when it comes to babyware is their effort to go green, especially when it comes to nappies. In Leicestershire alone about 50 million nappies are thrown away each year, and their landfills are brimming with them. To combat this problem, the city is pushing "sustainable babyware." In this case, reusable nappies. To promote awareness, the city led a campaign in which their taxis were painted purple and donned with a picture of a baby in a striped disposable nappy with the claim that switching to these will save each consumer 700 pounds ($968) a year.

Natter

There's nothing like a good natter on the phone, and the best natterers, of course, talk **nineteen to the dozen.** It's a happy little word, probably from *gnatter,* a northern dialect word.

Although honest in its hint of "endless chattering," it is nevertheless forgiving and approving at the same time. So it's yet another of those English terms for little human weaknesses that make life worth living (*see also* "Flutter").

Naughts and Crosses

Whether it's Exy-Ozys in Northern Ireland, X's and O's in Canada and Scotland, or Tic-Tac-Toe in America, this simple kids game, in which the object is to get three in a row lined up in a grid before your opponent does, remains the most common outlet for students bored in class. The earliest known variant of this game originated in the Roman Empire in the first century B.C.

And the game's outcome is as consistent as its history—nearly always a draw.

Nice cup of tea

Reports say that Britons drink somewhere between 130 and 160 million cups of tea a day, though it's not clear who is counting them.

It is comforting, however, for all those tea lovers, so long considered unsexy, to read *the Londonpaper*'s report of November 28, 2006, that "tea is the new coffee." It seems that with the approval of stellar names such as Kate Moss, Daniel Craig, and Stella McCartney, the paper says, "tea houses are fast becoming the place to be seen in the capital."

The celebrity tea habit goes back to the seventeenth century in England when, in imitation of the racy and liberal tea-drinking monarch Charles II, tea houses sprang up in London and became the fashionable venue for the sophisticated.

As for "a nice cup of tea," well, that's another matter. The Japanese do it their way, with ritual and ceremony, but do not think that the English are any less fussy. There is tea, and then there is "a nice cup of tea." To show how seriously this matter is taken, the great novelist and essayist George Orwell published a postwar article (*Evening Standard*, January 12, 1946) entitled A NICE CUP OF TEA, where he asserts that "tea is one of the mainstays of civilization in this country." When he looks through his own recipe for tea, he says, "I find no fewer than 11 outstanding points," and goes on to enumerate his rules, "every one of which I regard as golden."

In its generic form tea is quite classless, yet if we examine the practice of tea making at an average truck stop (as they say, a spoon will stand up in it) compared to the beverage served by Lady Muck-Worthington to the local vicar, there is a world of difference. "Just my/your cup of tea" expresses without ambiguity what your taste is, whether in things, places, or people. "Surrey is a very different cup of tea from Kent," reinforces a contrast. And in the form "Not my cup of tea," we hear a very English type of judgment— not too severe, not too condemnatory, but firm and telling all the same.

Nineteen to the dozen

This saying goes all the way back to the eighteenth century, but its origin is unclear. The sense suggests something happening much faster than the average and most often refers to speech—hence, "she talked nineteen to the dozen."

The parallel expression "ten to the dozen" is used, illogically, in the same sense. One unconvincing source sometimes quoted comes from the introduction of steam pumps to Cornish mines, where their speed of operation cleared 19,000 gallons of water for every 12 bushels of coal burned. A similar colorful phrase for fast talking, and equally obscure in its origin, is "to talk the hind legs off a donkey."

Nowt so queer as folk

A recent antidote to the complicated world we live in has been found in the robust cheerfulness of northern English people. As the subject of a number of popular films and TV series, they have displayed a strong sense of community, straightforward speech, a sense of humor, and a philosophy of keeping their feet on the ground.

There is no sexual reference as far as this saying goes; it simply states the obvious but frequently forgotten truth that "there's nothing so strange as people." And while we're on the subject, a moment to reflect on the classic northern observation that "all the world's mad save thee and me; and even thee's a little queer."

Oh, yes he did!

Almost any child in England will recognize this catch-phrase from the pantomime, that traditional end-of-year family outing without which Christmas just wouldn't be Christmas. It comes during a typically noisy to-and-fro between the stage and the audience, in which the one contradicts the other, louder and louder each time: *"Oh, yes he did!" "Oh, no he didn't!"*

Pantomime—a mixture of dialogue, song, and dance, usually with added stage effects—came to England from the Italian *commedia dell'arte,* a form of street theater that traveled around fairs and festivals. Its stock characters include a pretty heroine looking for a husband, a good but simple young man, a dame who acts as friend and protectress and, most important, a villain whose sole object is to frustrate their happiness. One peculiarity of the casting (hard to explain to visitors) is that the principal boy is always a girl in tights, and the dame is played by a man in a bonnet and flouncy dress.

Nowadays a whole range of fairy-tale plots—Cinderella, Jack and the Beanstalk, Aladdin, Puss-in-Boots—are used as the basic story, which in its essence never changes. As in the old Italian tradition, the scriptwriters add in ridiculous jokes and allusions to current events and celebrities. There is much slapstick, improvisation, and innuendo, and at every point the audience is encouraged to join in the fun.

With its spontaneity, absurdity, and over-the-top vulgarity, pantomime is probably the closest thing the English have to what theater used to be like in the days before it was taken over by highbrow culture vultures.

Old Blighty

An affectionate term for Britain, Old Blighty—sometimes just "Blighty"—comes from military slang dating from the Indian campaigns of the nineteenth century. Blighty was the British soldier's corruption of the Hindi word *bilayati,* meaning "foreign." In their Anglo-Indian dictionary of 1886, Yule and Burnell say that the word was used to refer to a number of unfamiliar products that the English brought with them.

The expression came into common use as a term for Britain at the beginning of the First World War. It is nearly always associated with the soldier's sense of loss

and nostalgia for the "old country" and turns up in popular marching songs. It appears, too, in the lines of war
poets such as Siegfried Sassoon and Wilfred Owen, most
poignantly in the latter's poem "The Dead-Beat," where
a soldier in the trenches goes into a state of shock and
refuses to move, staring into nothing. A low voice says,
"It's Blighty, p'raps, he sees."

Old school tie

George Bernard Shaw once wrote that "it is impossible
for an Englishman to open his mouth without making
some other Englishman hate him."

Although some would have us believe that the English
class system is dead and buried, a different story is told by
the huge number of judgmental words used to describe
English people who are perceived to be of a different
class to the speaker. The "old school tie" connection is a
case in point—a reference to the practice of members of
the upper classes showing favor to others simply because
they went to the "right" school; that is, a very expensive
one and, quite by chance, the same school as themselves.

On the pull

One of those English terms that can baffle Americans,
though the basic practice is not unfamiliar. It is a truth
universally acknowledged that single men and women
are in constant search of the ideal partner, and therefore
part of the social game is to go out hunting. But unlike
in other centuries, when brute force or wealth alone

brought about success in this area, the modern hunt takes place in the absurd hope that somehow your personality will display irresistible magnetic properties, preferably for someone so attractive that they would normally never look at you. Thus, to be "on the pull" is to live in a continuing state of self-delusion and unfounded optimism.

Oxbridge

Familiarly known as Oxbridge, Oxford and Cambridge need no introduction as world-famous centers of tradition and excellence, always in a certain tension and competition with one another, always top of the game in the lure they have for candidates leaving school and going on to university.

Where would England be without Oxbridge, either to love or condemn for its undisputed image of privilege and prestige? For many its picture of gilded youth is still the blissful dreamy setting of the pages of Evelyn Waugh's *Brideshead Revisited*, an endless summer of college gardens, boating, riverside pubs, and genial servants clearing up the mess after one's excesses. But those days are long gone, and the fictional descriptions always forgot to mention the ferociously cold winter climate of both cities, together with the harsh reality of living in medieval buildings without any plumbing.

The plumbing these days has much improved, and along with that and other modernizing influences, the exquisitely photogenic background has become more adapted to the down-to-earth thoughts of grumpy yet

beloved fictional detective Inspector Morse than the quails' egg breakfasts enjoyed by Sebastian Flyte of *Brideshead Revisited*.

In the real world, Oxbridge continues to represent a time of forging connections and friendships for life, and with competition for jobs ever more severe, it may ease the path to a career after graduating, if a career is really what you want after such an exalted education (see "Old school tie").

Peckish

As in the States, the English are fighting high obesity rates. Most people are less active than they used to be, rely more on **takeaway** due to their busy lifestyles, and are "pecking" at more snacks and sweets than they care to admit. With this discovery, the English are changing their ways, and according to recent government statistics, the British diet is probably as healthy as it's ever been and their intake of saturated fat is decreasing in line with government targets.

But this hasn't solved any issue of their feeling peck-ish—somewhat annoyed, irritable, or hungry. This term goes back to 1785. Hundreds of websites offer ways to overcome feeling peckish by offering tips on healthy snacks, like granola and fruit. Annoyed yet?

People like us

Often abbreviated to PLU, this phrase is used by those of a certain social class to approve of others as acceptable by birth and station and originates in the 1940s milieu typified by the artistic, wayward, and eccentric Mitford sisters, daughters of the second Baron Redesdale. We get a taste of the attitude where Nancy Mitford, in a letter to her sister Jessica (August 28, 1957), declared that "People Like Us are never killed in earthquakes."

Nancy refined the art of social-class distinctions in her book *Noblesse Oblige* with a list of subtle differences in vocabulary first defined as U (upper class) and non-U (aspriring middle class) by the sociolinguist Alan Ross in 1954. For U openers, we have napkin, bike, rich, jam (jelly), and lavatory; while non-U gives us serviette, cycle, wealthy, preserve, and toilet. These may seem arbitrary, but they bear the daily truth that in England your speech betrays your social category. In reality, of course, U people will often instantly identify your place in society by your shoes or the cut of your clothes. Similarly, in a famous putdown, a Conservative Party grandee said of a self-made colleague: "He bought all his own furniture," implying that anyone of class would naturally inherit such things.

Pint of bitter

As the rest of Europe knows all too well, England (in the form of the U.K. government) has fought hard to keep certain traditions untouched by the bureaucratic hand of Brussels.

Well, if the French can do it for cheese and farmers, why can't the English do it for beer, their national drink? And so the pint of bitter, with its popular blend of hops and malt, continues to be served in English pubs in defiance of metrication.

In September 2007, after years of wrangling and complaining, the European Commission finally gave up the struggle. Gunter Verheugen, the EU Industry Commissioner, declared: "I want to bring to an end a bitter, bitter battle that has lasted for decades and which in my view is completely pointless." He seems to have been completely unaware of the dreadful pun on "bitter" in his statement.

Yet beer-drinking habits have undergone much change in recent years, according to a 2008 survey from brewery giant SABMiller. This is mainly due to long working hours for the English, as many work up to 48 hours per week. Regular lunchtime drinking is a thing of the past, with only 1 in 10 Britons enjoying a midday pint. And they start drinking later in the evening than any of their European neighbors. To be precise, at 6:14 P.M., the report says. Research is a wonderful tool, to discover these things with such accuracy.

Ploughman's lunch

This well-known phrase from English pub menus has an attractive ring to it, intentionally. In reality meaning nothing more than "bread and cheese," garnished with a bit of salad, it conjures up the hearty fare of country inns and images of the rugged countryman and his healthy lifestyle. But we find a darker layer to the phrase in the 1983 film *The Ploughman's Lunch,* written by Ian MacEwan.

Here a young journalist from a humble background rises socially in a world dominated by cold-hearted commerce and right-wing economics. During a pub meal with a friend, the term "ploughman's lunch" is exposed as a mere marketing label to sell a simple product at an inflated price. The book is an ironic and bleak comment on how modern commercial practices that threaten an older pattern of English life exploit terms like "traditional," "country," and "home" in their advertising and labeling.

Posh

Port **o**ut, **s**tarboard **h**ome—*posh*—was the preferred ship cabin to occupy on the long sea journey out to India in the days of the Raj, because those sides of the ship suffered less from the heat of direct sunlight on the corresponding journey. Clearly, passengers with more social importance and higher incomes booked the preferred cabins.

The term came into more general use to describe anyone with money and a certain social background. Only the genuine social article was "posh," the newly rich being considered a lesser and more vulgar breed. The truly posh rose effortlessly to become members of government and captains of industry, mostly through the **old school tie** network and then a typically Oxford or Cambridge education, where relationships with their own kind were forged for life (see "Oxbridge"). Among so-called public schools (in reality, expensive and private), centuries-old institutions such as Eton, Harrow, and Winchester continue to represent the most select places for educating youngsters for the hardships of wealthy adulthood.

It need hardly be said that the privileged upper classes do not use the term of themselves. "Posh" was always how the lower social classes saw both them and their lifestyle, thus conveying a strange mixture of resentment, envy, and admiration.

The twentieth century, of course, saw a great social leveling, and the last 50 years especially have witnessed the growing realization in England of the American dream—that anyone from any background can become anything he wants. But no matter how rich and important you might rise to be, you can never become posh. The distinction persists in English society to this day, though the influence of the "posh class" has dramatically waned.

Pottering

Pottering is not a hobby. Do not be misled into thinking it means filling your time in trifling ways. Pottering is a national occupation. English people go to work to earn money so they can come home and potter. However (and this is why they have to earn the money), you need a garden to potter in. A piece of English earth that is your own. This is every English person's dream.

So when you hear that fine-sounding expression "An Englishman's home is his castle," it actually means "An Englishman's garden is his castle." No feature of English life gives more happiness and sense of security, or more tension with one's neighbors. A garden is an oasis that is the complete expression of your own personality, to be defended at all costs from every type of threat around, including Mr. Smith's cat, Mrs. Johnson's terrier, and Mr. Smith and Mrs. Johnson themselves.

Quite clearly, though, the primeval enemy of the suburban garden is Nature itself (but see "ha-ha" for other attitudes), and this is where pottering becomes a vital pursuit. As we say, the price of freedom is eternal vigilance. Nature must be watched at all times. So pottering is a kind of routine security procedure, demanding the closest attention to very small things like ants and beetles, as well as to the activities of larger enemies, such as rabbits, moles, squirrels, and pigeons. No stone must be left unturned in the search for slugs, no flowering border left unexamined in case an alien creature has penetrated into the sanctuary.

A lifetime can be spent improving the boundary defenses, constructing paths that enable you to rush to the site of an emergency, putting up conservatories so that you can keep up a 24-hour watch. All of this is very costly in terms of time and money, but absolutely essential for English national security. (For more gardening wisdom, see "Chelsea.")

Queen's speech

The relationship between the royal family and television
has had a somewhat checkered history. Queen Elizabeth
II's reign began with a TV event, since her coronation in
June 1953 was the first major national occasion to be tele-
vised. The Queen went on to deliver a television message
to the nation every Christmas, from 1957 onward. This was
a speech read out in a live broadcast as the Queen sat in a
chair in front of the camera and was famous for its stiff for-
mality and the oft repeated phrase "My husband and I...."

Over the years, advisers encouraged the Queen to
relax the style of her presentation, and she began to present more of a pictorial record of the year, with her voice
as background commentary. We now have it from academic studies that the Queen's pronunciation also shifted
with time and is now much closer to a popular accent
than the so-called "cut-glass" accent of the upper classes of
yore. Jonathan Harrington and colleagues at Macquarie
University, Sydney, wrote in their 2000 study:

> Our analysis reveals that the Queen's pronunciation
> of some vowels has been influenced by the standard

southern British [SSB] accent of the 1980s, which is more typically associated with speakers younger and lower in the social hierarchy.... We conclude that the Queen no longer speaks the Queen's English of the 1950s, although the vowels of the 1980s Christmas message are still clearly set apart from those of an SSB accent.

In an update, published in the *Journal of Phonetics* of December 2006, Harrington said:

The changes also reflect the changing class struc-ture over the last 50 years. In the 1950s, there was a much sharper distinction between the classes as well as accents that typified them. Since then, the class boundaries have become more blurred, and so have the accents. Fifty years ago, the idea that Queen's English could be influenced by cockney would have been unthinkable.

Queer

This innocent-looking little adjective is an explosive device in a social minefield. It arrived in English in the sixteenth century from the German word *quer* (oblique) and originally meant different from normal, or strange. Then it came to mean unwell. Older fiction sometimes had characters feeling or "coming over" queer.

Children's author Enid Blyton (1897–1968), whose lexi-cal range was not huge, had characters feeling queer on almost every page of her *Famous Five* and other books. Then in the 1950s, long before the homosexual community came out and adopted the jolly term "gay," queer turned into a derogatory term for a homosexual man. Although gay people themselves sometimes now use the word in expressions such as queer cinema and queer politics, this problematic word is best avoided in normal conversation.

Queue

It isn't clear why English people form an orderly queue for almost every occasion, while those on the **Continent** do not. But as we have already seen, the Continent is "a foreign country: they do things differently there." Perhaps it is that the English display a mixture of diffidence and fairness, both profoundly English qualities, in their attitude to queuing. On the one hand, they hate to push themselves forward—that would make themselves conspicuous and therefore very **un-English**—and on the other hand, they recognize the right of those who come first to claim their place.

The corollary to the queuing theory is that queue jumpers are never challenged but only silently regarded with the contempt they deserve.

Quite

Along with "rather," quite is one of those qualifying words that typically expresses English reservation and unwillingness to overstate anything—or, as their enemies might add, to say anything very clearly at all. I am *quite* sure they are wrong, however, as even the word "quite," as here exemplified, can have a gently, modestly, undramatically reinforcing value as well. When an Englishman is quite sure, you can be certain he is very sure.

Raining cats and dogs

No book on England would be complete without mentioning the weather, and that green and pleasant land owes much of its greenness and pleasantness to rain. As many a visitor discovers, an English summer is no guarantee of sun. At any time, a downpour can wash out a picnic or a sporting event, and whether Wimbledon or Lords, the rain shows a total disrespect for international tennis and cricket. But I imagine that Shakespeare's original open-air Globe theater frequently suffered the same fate, perhaps inspiring Feste's lament at the end of *Twelfth Night* that "the rain it raineth every day."

The English spend a lot of time wondering about rain—Will it? Won't it?—and complaining about it when it does. Rain for them commands a wide range of vocabulary, including drizzle, shower, spit, pour, deluge, pelt, torrent, cloudburst, downpour, as well as the more graphic metaphors, to rain buckets, stair rods, pitchforks, and then cats and dogs. The buckets are plain enough, stair rods and pitchforks one can more or less imagine, but cats and dogs?

There is an early seventeenth-century reference to rain-ing "dogs and polecats," and some 90 years later Jonathan Swift gives us "He was sure it would rain cats and dogs." The origin of the expression is obscure. Could it really come from Norse sea lore associating the spirits of cats with rain, and dogs with wind? Unlikely. Or is it rhym-ing slang for "raining frogs"? Or, when it poured down in earlier times, did city dwellers literally see the streets awash with dead cats and dogs, as Swift's own "Description of a City Shower" tells us? There seems no better theory to offer than poor drainage and a plague of unfortunate stray animals.

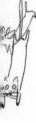

Red herring

We all know about the red her-ring in the plot of a detective novel, the misleading sugges-tion of a perpetrator and motive for the crime to throw us off the scent of the real killer. Red herrings, colored so by the process of salting and smoking, were a cheap form of food in the Middle Ages and, like kippers, had a particularly strong smell.

The belief is that because of this, they were used to mislead hunting dogs, by

being dragged across country. Whether this was to train
the dogs or was the dastardly work of some early Fox
Liberation Movement, isn't clear. But from this practice
came the meaning of "a false scent."

Right of way

The English do get bees in their bonnets about some things,
and the rights of the individual are high on that list. But
rather than the massive street demonstrations held on the
Continent, the English way is to go quietly about protect-
ing their rights with small but effective gestures. Almost
emblematic of the small man's struggle against oppression
is the issue of "rights of way," or public footpaths. Many of
these are centuries old and without vigilance can fall into
disuse or become blocked by landowners. The Ramblers
Association, founded in 1935 and now with some 140,000
members, campaigns for the right of walkers to access land
and coast, and in 2000 its efforts were crowned with some
success in establishing a "right to roam."

A hilarious representative of the individual pitted
against authority, society, and adversity in general was
English comic Tony Hancock, whose TV series *Hancock's
Half Hour* showed him grappling with big issues affecting
"the small man." From his modest home at 23 Railway
Cuttings, East Cheam, he sallied out to defend basic freedoms with limited education. One of his more famous
anguished lines went "Does Magna Carta mean nothing
to you? Did she die in vain?"

Serendipity

Serendipity is a made-up word, meaning the way in which we sometimes make happy but quite accidental discoveries. The English author Horace Walpole coined it in a letter written in 1754, saying he had based it on a Persian fairy tale called "The Three Princes of Serendip." He explained that the tale's heroes "were always making discoveries, by accidents and sagacity, of things they were not in quest of." Serendip is another form of Sarandip, the old Persian name for Sri Lanka. In spite of its exotic origins, the word suggests something of the happily amateur temperament of the English, which always seems to allow space for creativity to arise as if by chance.

Shandy

Shandy is a common abbreviation for "shandygaff," a beer mixed with lemonade or ginger beer, first recorded in the nineteenth century and of unknown origin. As a light, refreshing drink, it is popular with athletes. Note that the British mix is with ginger beer *not* ginger ale.

But probably more important with regard to the history of English words, Tristram Shandy is the eponymous hero and narrator of Laurence Sterne's riotous and confusing novel written in the eighteenth century as a broadside against rationalism. Sterne was born in Ireland but spent nearly all his life in England, for many years as a vicar in North Yorkshire. He adored playing with language and was also a compulsive lover and inventor of words, including *lackadaisical, whimsicality, muddle-headed, good-tempered,* and *sixth sense.* Writing for many years from the timeless tranquillity of Yorkshire villages, he left behind a legacy of **zany** wordplay and sheer zest for invention and innuendo, which has given us an entire genre of apparently extempore writing, exemplified by authors like James Joyce.

Sleeping policeman

Discouraging speeders is a high priority for English local authorities, intent on trying to reduce road accidents. And this means, essentially, putting a whole variety of obstacles in the path of cars so that they are forced to slow down. The amusingly named "sleeping policeman"

is a raised bump of asphalt placed across a road surface to deter speeding.

Having contributed so much to the spread of the high-revolution internal combustion engine, the English—at least at the level of the governing authorities—are now waging constant war against it.

Snarky

This term has two meanings, depending on who is on the receiving end. Some use it to describe someone who is irritable, short-tempered, or disrespectful; others view it as a more admirable quality, a sarcastic wit that can be so abrupt that it will amuse some and leave others in complete shock. This term goes back to the 1920s and is said to be a combination of sarcastic and nasty.

Soppy

The English have so many condemnatory words for the weak and ineffectual that you have to conclude their self-image is that of a people who are tough, resistant, and able to adapt to hardship. And that is *exactly* how they see themselves. When Mrs Thatcher, the Iron Lady, famously said to a minister, "Don't be so wet!" she struck a firm note with the public. "Wet" means "soppy," which means lacking resolution, the capacity to make hard decisions. In an interesting nuance, "soppy" also means "soft" in relationships, showing one's feelings too much, which of course is a very **un-English** thing to do.

Sorry

Elton John may have sung that "Sorry seems to be the hardest word," but for most English people the contrary is true. The word "sorry" is heard constantly as a mollifying disguise for grievance, in situations where you would normally expect the speaker to express anger or to be upset. Look out for: "I'm sorry, but there seems to be a fly in my soup," or "I'm sorry, but I've been waiting for over an hour to be served."

Because the English hate public embarrassment of any kind, they bend over backward to avoid making any direct accusation. So next time someone stands on your foot in a London crowd, you know exactly what to say: "Sorry!"

Spend a penny

Now here's a challenge for an American visitor to England. You ask your server for directions to the restroom, a polite way of saying you want to relieve yourself, and he stares at you blankly. What now?

Well, there are many euphemistic phrases for this most basic of human needs. The most familiar is to say, "Where is the ladies/gents, please?" Or you can use the upper classes' hygienic euphemism: "Where can I wash my hands?"

"To spend a penny" comes from the old practice, literally, of having to put a penny in the door of a public convenience. "To see a man about a dog" is an informal phrase that appears to go back to the mid-1800s and, in its earlier sense, meant to go and visit a woman sexually.

Stiff upper lip

"Stiff upper lip" denotes a quintessentially English outlook on life. It describes a very English way of reacting to life's little ups and downs: a much-admired quality of uncomplaining stoicism and composure under pressure. In many ways, it can be seen as an extension of the complicated social etiquette that English people hold so dear. The English will go to great lengths to "keep up appearances" and not draw attention to themselves, either by keeping quiet and soldiering on in the face of adversity, or by remaining polite, patient, and respectful, even when provoked.

Sweet Fanny Adams

This saying, unlike many, has a clear historical source, though its path to its current meaning of "absolutely nothing" has been rather circuitous. Poor Fanny Adams was the child victim of a murderer, her dismembered corpse being found in August 1867 in the town of Alton, England. Her tombstone is still there. Much public outrage and discussion surrounded the arrest and execution of her murderer, the child herself becoming widely known as Sweet Fanny Adams because of her age and innocence.

Around the same time, the Royal Navy introduced tinned meat rations, which sailors disliked and referred to as Sweet Fanny Adams in a grisly association with the child murder. As such, the expression spread into wider use as meaning something of little or no value.

Takeaway

This word refers to the eating establishment itself—a place that sells only food to take out—or the food that you buy there: "I just purchased some Indian takeaway" (see also "Chips"). Indian food gained popularity after World War II because of its low cost and great variety and has been a staple part of the national diet there for over 50 years. In fact, the country boasts over 8,000 Indian eating establishments, compared to only about 500 in 1960.

Thatcher and thatching

Mrs. Thatcher, Britain's first woman prime minister, was a greengrocer's daughter and, so journalists loved to tell us, ran the country on the same principles as a shop. However, an ancestor of a different trade is revealed by her surname, as with a wide array of English family names of trades, crafts, and occupations: cooper, brewer, fisher, carpenter, miller, smith, not to mention kemp (wrestler), fletcher (arrow maker), hayward (fencer), and keeler (bargeman).

Around the twelfth century, when the practice
of naming after occupations was firmly established,
Thatchers were plentiful. In England, unlike Scotland
or Wales, stone and slate were not available. Builders
depended on local resources such as woodlands, and
thatched roofs were commonplace. But once modern
transport allowed heavier materials like slate and bricks
to be carried all over the country, thatch fell out of favor.
Nowadays thatch is only the choice of those wanting to
preserve a picturesque, if expensive, reminder of that
"old world" so distant from their own times.

Toff

The *Oxford English Dictionary* places the origin of the
word "toff" in a corruption of "tuft," the gold tassel once
worn by titled undergraduates at Oxford and Cambridge
(see "Oxbridge"). To be sure, the label "toff" is not
intended to be a kind one. The suggestion is of someone
remote from the concerns and trials of ordinary people.
After all, to be a real toff is to be of privileged birth,
elegantly dressed, careless with wealth, and probably
inclined toward boisterous behavior when out drinking
with fellow toffs.

Turned out nice again

We established earlier (see "Dog's life") that walking
around in public with a dog allows people to talk casu-
ally to strangers and therefore be quite **un-English.** But
what recourse is available to the Englishman who does

not have a dog? At any moment, he may pass a neighbor in the street or someone he recognizes, even if he can't quite remember their name or who they are. One cannot simply stare at the sidewalk, so what *can* he say that will safely mean absolutely nothing? He must talk about the weather—"Turned out nice again"—then stride on. And so the danger is past.

And what was the danger, exactly? The danger was that the person might just be one of those who, despite all the rules, wants to draw you into conversation and talk endlessly about their latest woes or, worse, ask you searching personal questions about your life, hopes, and anxieties.

Twitcher

Scientifically known as ornithology, bird-watching is far too serious to be called a hobby. It requires enormous patience, as well as the endurance to be very still and quiet for long periods of time. Having all these qualities, unlike their continental cousins, the English are perfectly suited for bird-watching.

The truly fanatical bird-watcher—one who rushes in with binoculars when a rare bird is spotted—is called a "twitcher."

U, V, W

Umming and erring

It's clear that the English love to **natter** on the phone, and
a recent report from BT, the British telephone company,
revealed that the average U.K. household spends 58.5 hours
on the telephone every year. But the study also showed that
about 10 percent of that time is made up of pure waffle,
what linguists call "filler words."

These exist in most languages but seem especially
marked in English speakers as *er, erm, um, you know, well,
actually, basically, know what I mean?* Psychological expert
Phillip Hodson, who carried out the research, comments:

> This BT study reveals Britain to be a nation of
> wafflers ... The descendants of Shakespeare, the
> guardians of the Oxford English Dictionary, have
> become lazier conversationalists ... Every 24 hours,
> a talker in Britain might use up to 10,000 redundant
> or "filler" words, or word repetitions. This amounts
> to about seven wasted words per minute, and only 10
> seconds pass before we relapse into further waffle.

Un-English

Another book would be needed to say what is "un-English," for it seems the English are defined as much by what they wouldn't dream of doing as by what they actually do. Such inhibition gives them kinship with other cultures, like the Japanese, where correctness rules. English sense and sensibility are renowned, and yet many of their fellow Europeans see their behavior, dress, and eating habits as uncouth. But it is not un-English to be badly dressed, rowdy in conversation, or to eat junk food. English rules are supposed to govern other things: emotions, confidences, openness, familiarity, and privacy. And yet, as the following entry shows, it isn't as simple as that, after all.

Valentine's Day

Valentine's Day observance in England has adopted a curious form absent in the rest of Europe and America. All those reserved and uptight English people, who, so we believe, can only ever talk obliquely of love and sex, fill the personal columns of newspapers with love messages phrased in language of the most intimate kind. In 2003 *The Times* (where the first Valentine's Day page appeared in 1975) reported that "today we have a Snuggle Bum and a Cute Bum, an Oogie Wag-wag and a Mr Nogsworth." And that is just a small part of the terms of endearment, nicknames, pillow talk, confessions of love to complete strangers, love verse, and worse.

Vicars and vulgarity

"More tea, vicar?" For most English people, if someone suddenly comes out with that line, it will be thought funny or at least raise a smile. We may ask, What is funny about it? But as soon as we ask, it stops being funny. This is because the English sense of humor has not so much to do with what is said, but rather with their attitude to life in general.

Basically, the more important the topic, the more likely they are to be humorous about it. Vicars are pillars of society, and on those grounds alone they are intrinsically funny. In English sitcoms male vicars are usually gentle, fussy individuals with good manners and intentions. They tend not to see or hear unpleasant things.

Nobody really knows anymore where the line came from. But it can be imagined in the setting of a visit to a local parishioner for tea, a small event reflecting social life in a village. Something has occurred to upset the neat order of the household. It is likely to be something quite vulgar. So the lady of the house feels the need to cover up and preserve the delicacy of the moment: "More tea, vicar?" Vicars and vulgarity—the two extremes produce quite a spark.

WAGs

Newspaper editors have contributed a lot to shaping the English language into short, witty headlines—and to creating new meanings at the same time. Once, we thought we knew what a "wag" was: Someone who likes telling funny stories. But now WAGs are "wives and girlfriends," usually of millionaire footballers (soccer players). These charming companions of sporting heroes turn up at major events as if on a fashion parade. Some are already famous in their own right, like Victoria Beckham, or Cheryl Cole of the group Girls Aloud. Others have been plucked from relative obscurity, where they worked as waitresses, personal trainers, or beauticians. Now they compete for the attention of the cameras in their designer clothes, flashy (mainly) fake tans, and diamond accessories. All those assets plus a big, handsome man with a luxury pad in Liverpool, Cheshire, or Mayfair should be enough to make any girl smile when the photographers call for it.

Warts and all

This saying goes back to a time when portraits of the great and good were usually painted with some discretion, the main object being to disguise the uglier features of the sitter. This would always have been the case with royal portraits. But when the new Lord Protector, Oliver Cromwell, the Puritan parliamentarian who overthrew King Charles I, was having his portrait done around 1657, he insisted that the artist, Sir Peter Lely, should not flatter him at all but show "all the roughness, pimples, warts and everything as you see me, otherwise I will never pay you a farthing for it."

So it was to be, with the portrait now on display in Bolton Art Gallery, showing a large wart below Cromwell's mouth.

Wellies

The Duke of Wellington was the first to take the standard so-called Hessian boot, fashionable for the military in the eighteenth century, and redesign it to his own taste. What he came up with was thereafter known as the "Wellington boot," a soft leather mid-calf design that was both practical for daywear and comfortable enough for evenings in the field.

What the English have now come to call "wellies" are a tough waterproof version of the Duke's boots, suitable for walking over wet and muddy ground, and standard wear for country dwellers. "Green welly brigade" is a slightly mocking term for middle- and upper-class "weekender" country folk who disdain the normal black boots used by people actually working on the land.

With respect

One of those confusing little English expressions that, in fact, means exactly the opposite of the words used (*see also* "Don't mind me!" and "Sorry").

XXXX words

In 1965, for the first time ever, critic Kenneth Tynan used a sexual four-letter word on British TV, and motions of censure were signed by over a hundred members of Parliament. The BBC had to issue a formal apology. Eleven years later suspensions followed the Sex Pistols' swearing on ITV's *Today* show. These days, with reality TV taking over, controls are impossible, and thus the boundaries of propriety are moving.

It's interesting, then, to note that today's **XXXX** words are not so much sexual as social. In recent times broadcasters have been scolded for uttering terms like pikey, chav, and **toff** in derogatory contexts referring to social categories. Historically, pikeys were turnpike travelers of gypsy origin and long seen as fringe people. Chav is a Romany word meaning "lad" but has recently become associated with a brand of surly, tasteless youth culture.

Debating the use of these terms, along with jibes such as "pleb" and "prole," some see a resurgence of social tension in England. Others say that political correctness has gone too far. "Ban pikey," wrote Des Kelly in the *Daily Mail* (June 9, 2008), "and you might as well outlaw chav, townie, trailer trash, Hooray Henry, goth, Sloane, tinker, and many more fairly innocuous labels."

Yours sincerely

Author Henry Hitchings, who is referred to as a master of the English language and who recently wrote *The Secret Life of Words: How the English became English,* reports that John Gay, author of *The Beggars' Opera*, "seems to have been the first letter-writer to sign off 'Yours sincerely.'" The phrase has certainly caught on since then, more formally than in a spirit of genuine sincerity, and again invites the comment that the English, like the Japanese, use language to smooth over social situations where telling the plain truth is simply not done (see "With respect").

Zany

As we have seen, English borrows terms from wherever it likes and uses them for its own purposes. Zany, for example, was confirmed in the eighteenth century as a thoroughly English word by Samuel Johnson himself. In his day it was mostly used as a noun meaning, in his definition, a "merry andrew" or "buffoon." But the term actually came from Italian entertainment in which a character known as "Zanni," derived from Giovanni, aped the words and behavior of the principal players.

Nowadays it is used as an adjective to describe one who indulges in harmless tomfoolery, raising laughs by going beyond the bounds.

Zed

Zed comes from the original Greek *zeta* by way of the Old French *zede*, and pretty much all Englishmen pronounce it this way. According to the *Concise Oxford Companion*, "The modification of zed ... to zee appears to have been by analogy with bee, dee, vee, etc." *Lye's New Spelling Book* (1677) was the first to list "zee" as a correct pronunciation, and Webster confirmed it in 1827. Many believe the distinction sprang up shortly after the Revolution in an effort to sound **un-English** and vice versa, but it is hard to imagine that "thou whoreson Zed, thou unneccessary letter," as Shakespeare so eloquently states in *The Tragedy of King Lear*, could bequeath so much power.

Bibliography

Andrews, R., J. Brown, R. Humphreys, and P. Lee. *The Rough Guide to England.* U.K.: Rough Guides, 2008.

Austen, Jane. *Northanger Abbey.* London: John Murray, 1817.

Barone, James. "Comparing apples and oranges: a randomised prospective study." *British Medical Journal*; 23 December 2000; 321(7276): 1569–1570).

Brewer, E. Cobham. *Dictionary of Phrase and Fable.* Philadelphia: Henry Altemus,1898.

Bryson, Bill. *Mother Tongue: The English Language.* U.K.: Penguin, 1999.

Chaucer, Geoffrey, *The Riverside Chaucer.* Oxford: Oxford University Press, 2008.

Forster, E. M. *A Room with a View.* U.K.: Edward Arnold, 1908.

Fowler H. W. and F. G. Fowler. *The King's English.* Oxford: Clarendon Press, 1908.

Fox, Adam. *Oral and Literate Culture in England.* Oxford: Oxford University Press, 2000.

Fox, Kate. *Watching the English: The Hidden Rules of English Behaviour.* U.K.: Hodder and Stoughton, 2005.

Gower, John. *Confessio Amantis.* U.K.: The Echo Library, 2007.

Harrington, J., S. Palethorpe and C. Watson. "Does the Queen Speak the Queen's English?" *Nature.* 21 December 2000; (408) 927–928.

Jerome, Jerome K. *Three Men in a Boat.* U.K.: J. W. Arrowsmith, 1889.

Jonson, Ben. "Timber: or, Discoveries" (1641). *The Works of Ben Jonson*, viii. 625, eds. C. H. Herford and Percy Simpson. Oxford: 1925–52.

Johnson, Samuel. *Dr. Johnson's Dictionary.* U.K.: Penguin Classics, 2005.

Kelly, Stan. "The Liverpool Lullaby," recorded by Cilla Black, 1969.

Kipling, Rudyard. *The Complete Verse.* London: Kyle Cathie, 2006.

Newbolt, Henry. *Collected Poems of Henry Newbolt.* U.K.: Thomas Nelson & Sons, 1907.

Pepys, Samuel. *The Diaries of Samuel Pepys—A Selection.* U.K.: Penguin Classics, 2003.

Pliny the Elder. *Natural History: A Selection.* Trans. John Healey. U.K.: Penguin Classics, 2004. Print.

Quinion, Michael. www.worldwidewords.org (456); 27 August 2005.

Sellers, Peter and Sophia Loren. "Bangers and Mash," 1961.

Shakespeare, William. *The Complete Works of William Shakespeare.* U.K.: Wordsworth Editions Ltd., 1996. Print.

Shaw, Bernard. *Pygmalion.* New York: Brentano, 1916.

Sheldrake, Rupert. *Seven Experiments That Could Change the World.* U.S.: Riverhead Books, 1996.

Sheridan, Richard. *The Rivals.* U.K.: Nick Hern Books, 1994. Print.

Sterne, Laurence. *The Life and Opinions of Tristram Shandy, Gentleman.* U.K.: Penguin, 1998.

Wilde, Oscar. *The Complete Works of Oscar Wilde.* U.K.: Collins, 2003. Print.

Wilson Thomas, *Art of Rhetorique*, (1553). Oxford: Benediction Classics, 2007. Print.

Yeats, W. B. *The Collected Poems of W. B. Yeats.* U.K.: Wordsworth Editions, 2000. Print.

ENJOY THESE OTHER
READER'S DIGEST BESTSELLERS

A Certain Je Ne Sais Quoi

A smorgasbord of foreign words and phrases used in everyday English—from aficionado (Spanish) to zeitgeist (German). Inside you'll find translations, definitions, and origins that will delight and amuse language lovers everywhere.

Chloe Rhodes
ISBN 978-1-6065-2057-4

My Grammar and I... Or Should That Be Me?

Confused about when to use "its" or "it's" or the correct spelling of "principal" or "principle"? Avoid language pitfalls and let this entertaining and practical guide improve both your speaking and writing skills.

Caroline Taggart & J. A. Wines
ISBN 978-1-60652-026-0

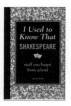

I Used to Know That: Shakespeare

Capturing the unbelievable scope of Shakespeare's influence, this book will surprise and delight you not only with fascinating facts and little-known details of his life but also with the surprising legacy of the language and phrases inherited from his works.

Liz Evers
ISBN 978-1-60652-246-2

Opening Pandora's Box

Engaging and fun, this little book pries the lid off the English language and reveals the secrets behind hundreds of timeless everyday expressions whose origins spring from the Greeks and Romans.

Ferdie Addis
ISBN 978-1-60652-324-7

Each book is $14.95 hardcover.

For more information visit us at RDTradePublishing.com
E-book editions also available.

Reader's Digest books can be purchased through retail and online bookstores.
In the United States books are distributed by Penguin Group (USA), Inc.
For more information or to order books, call 1-800-788-6262.